ABC of women workers' rights and gender equality

DATE DUE			

13FL03498

**344.01
ABC**

**ABC of women
workers' rights and
gender equality.**

**GAVIT MIDDLE/HIGH SCHOOL
HAMMOND, INDIANA**

ABC of women workers' rights and gender equality

Second edition

International Labour Office Geneva

ILO
ABC of women workers' rights and gender equality
Geneva, International Labour Office, 2000

Woman worker, women's rights, equal employment opportunity, ILO Convention, ILO Recommendation, comment. 14.04.2

ISBN 978-92-2-119622-8

ILO Cataloguing-in-Publication Data

Photocomposed in Switzerland   BRI
Printed in Switzerland   PCL

Contents

Preface

This publication expands on previous versions of the *ABC of women workers' rights and gender equality* and incorporates important International Labour Organization (ILO) instruments that have emerged since its last revision, such as the Resolution on gender equality, pay equity and maternity protection adopted at the 92nd Session of the International Labour Conference in 2004.

Non-discrimination and the promotion of equality have been fundamental principles underpinning the work of the ILO since its creation in 1919. These principles are an integral component of the ILO's Decent Work Agenda – promoting decent and productive work in conditions of freedom, equity, security and human dignity – and are also inherent to the Millennium Development Goals. All workers have the right to decent work, not only those working in the formal economy, but also the self-employed, casual and informal economy workers, as well as those, predominantly women, working in the care economy and private households.

International labour standards are one of the ILO's primary means of action to improve the working and living conditions of women and men, and promote equality in the workplace for all workers. All ILO standards, with some exceptions, in particular those addressing issues relating to maternity and women's reproductive role, apply equally to men and women. However, there continues to be a gap between the rights set out in national and international standards and the real situation of workers. These rights must be made effective in practice. A major obstacle preventing workers from exercising their rights is a lack of awareness of their existence. Dissemination of information about these rights is, therefore, a vital instrument for improving gender equality. This publication is one element in that dissemination process.

The ILO hopes that the information provided in this second *ABC of women workers' rights and gender equality* will contribute further to maintaining commitment to gender equality in the world of work and enhancing knowledge of the issues concerned with it, and will encourage and empower those who feel discriminated against to defend their rights.

The *ABC of women workers' rights and gender equality* owes its existence to a large number of dedicated colleagues whose insight has been invaluable in finalizing the preceding and current editions. The previous versions took shape under the supervision of Eugenia Date-Bah and Jane Zhang with technical input and support from Ingeborg Heide, Simonetta Cavazza, Mara Steccazzini and Petra

Ulshoefer. This second and expanded edition was expertly and patiently produced by Mandy Macdonald. Acknowledgement goes to the many technical departments and units in the ILO who contributed to the various entries. Particular thanks go to Jane Hodges, Shauna Olney, Karin Klotzbuecher, Naomi Cassirer and Anne Trebilcock for their overall comments and input. Geir Tonstol took the initiative for the revision and coordinated the process.

This publication aims to be an accessible guide to international labour standards relevant to women workers' rights and the promotion of gender equality in the world of work, based on a wide reading of ILO documentation and consultation with numerous experts on the topics. However, it does not necessarily reflect the agreed definitions or the official views of the Organization.

This revision has been undertaken with support from the Governments of Sweden and Denmark.

Evy Messell
Director, Bureau for Gender Equality
International Labour Office

Introduction: Labour standards promoting women workers' rights and gender equality

1. How to use this guide

The ILO considers it extremely important to increase knowledge of the legal aspects of gender equality in the world of work. While legal instruments for promoting gender equality and protecting women workers' rights are steadily expanding in number and being improved at both national and international levels, there is still a gap between the rights set out in national and international standards and their implementation in real situations. Even the best legal provisions cannot be of much use if they are not known and not put into practice. People need knowledge about legal rights and the machinery to enforce them if they are to combat discrimination and fight for a fair balance of opportunity, treatment, pay and representation between men and women in all areas of paid and unpaid employment and in work-related decision-making. However, many workers around the world are only hazily aware or even unaware of their rights, and this is perhaps the greatest obstacle to their exercising those rights.

This practical guide is intended to bridge that knowledge gap. Arranged alphabetically by topic, it focuses primarily on States' and employers' obligations and workers' rights as regards equality between men and women, enshrined in the ILO's body of international labour standards (Conventions and Recommendations). It also refers to other relevant developments and trends in international law (for example, United Nations instruments), supranational law (for instance, European Community directives), and national legislation and practice.

In addition, the guide includes explanations of a number of political, legal and socio-economic terms in common use and especially relevant to women workers and gender equality. These include, for instance, *Affirmative action*, *Export processing zones*, *Female-headed households*, the *Informal economy*, the *Glass ceiling*, and *Work–family balance*. There are also entries on law enforcement mechanisms and procedural rules, such as *Burden of proof*, and *Remedies and sanctions*. Terms and concepts relating to gender equality and its promotion, such as *Gender analysis and planning* and *Gender mainstreaming*, are explained with specific reference to the world of work. This new edition also contains a number of new entries that reflect recent issues of concern to the ILO, some of which are the subject of new and revised standards since the publication of the previous edition of the *ABC*; these include *Forced labour, Human resources development*, the *Employment relationship*, and *Trafficking in persons*.

For each topic in the book, the relevant provisions of the principal instruments that apply to that topic are described. These instruments are listed at the end of each entry, together with cross-references to related topics included in this guide. The list of instruments included at the end of each entry is not exhaustive, and by referring to certain standards in a particular entry we are not excluding the applicability of other standards to that subject, or limiting the application of the standards mentioned to that subject exclusively.

In particular, the Discrimination (Employment and Occupation) Convention, 1958 (No. 111) is so wide in its application that it has not been cited under every topic to which it applies. Note that Conventions are referred to in abbreviated form: for example, "*C. 88: Employment Service, 1948*" means "the Employment Service Convention, 1948 (No. 88)", while "*R. 150: Human Resources Development, 1975*" means "the Human Resources Development Recommendation, 1975 (No. 150)".

In one or two cases, standards jointly developed and adopted by the ILO together with other UN agencies, such as the ILO/UNESCO Recommendation concerning the Status of Teachers (1966), have been cited; but instruments adopted more broadly by the United Nations, such as the Universal Declaration of Human Rights or the Convention on the Elimination of All Forms of Discrimination against Women, have not been cited because their applicability is overarching.

Status of ILO standards

The ILO's Governing Body has decided that some 70 Conventions and 76 Recommendations are considered to be up-to-date. These are the principal instruments promoted. Some other standards remain on the books and, in the case of Conventions, remain binding on ratifying States. In this book, therefore, we refer for the most part only to ILO standards that are categorized as up to date. Exceptions include the Maternity Protection (Revised) Convention, 1952 (No. 103) and the Indigenous and Tribal Populations Convention, 1957 (No. 107), which remain important in countries which have not yet ratified the newer standards on these issues.

Terminology

Specific words and phrases are used in the texts of international labour standards to reflect the binding character of a provision. Wording using formulations such as "each Member shall…" or "each worker shall receive…" creates a legal obligation and/or a legal right. Such legal effect generally arises only from ratification, although there are certain fundamental principles which may be regarded as entering the domain of law irrespective of ratification.

For States which are not bound because they have not ratified an instrument, the aims and content of the instruments should nevertheless serve as policy guidance. Expressions such as "ought to" or "should" have been used regularly throughout this guide to show that the provisions described may be binding for ratifying countries and not binding for others. Exemptions are made for fundamental principles and rights at work, which must be respected and promoted in all ILO member States (see section 4, p. 6).

Many labour standards still in force predate the relatively recent concern with gender-neutral language, that is, terminology that does not assume that the typical worker is a man. In some cases the language has been updated in revised standards, but some standards still refer to "workmen" and use "he" as the generic pronoun. Where a male pronoun is used in a non-gender-specific way, this should on the whole be interpreted to include workers of both sexes. The *Manual for drafting ILO instruments*, elaborated by the ILO's Office of the Legal Adviser (JUR), gives guidance on the use of gender-inclusive language when drafting standards (ILO, 2005a, paras 254 ff.) and there is further guidance on using gender-inclusive drafting in national legislation in the *Labour legislation guidelines* (see *Further resources*).

2. Gender equality in the ILO's mandate

Universal and lasting peace can develop only on the basis of social justice. This is declared in the preamble to the ILO's Constitution of 1919. Even at that time, immediately after the First World War, the protection of women and the principle of equal remuneration for work of equal value were highlighted as areas calling for immediate action. At Philadelphia, in 1944, the International Labour Conference adopted a Declaration, now an annex to the Constitution, which proclaims that "all human beings, irrespective of race, creed or sex, have the right to pursue both their material well-being and their spiritual development in conditions of freedom and dignity, of economic security and equal opportunity". The Declaration also states that "poverty anywhere constitutes a danger to prosperity everywhere".

Women workers' rights constitute an integral part of the values, principles and objectives that are at the core of the ILO's mandate to promote social justice and decent work – fairly paid, productive work carried out in conditions of freedom, equity, security and dignity. While constantly adhering to this goal, the approach has changed considerably, in response to the evolving roles of women and men in society. Perceptions of the "traditional" share of paid labour and unpaid family or care work have been, and are still, undergoing profound changes. The ILO has not only reacted to those societal changes but has also taken a leading role in shaping a more equal future in the world of work. It does this by:

- promoting gender equality through international labour standards;
- advocating for measurable progress toward gender equality with its constituents (governments, employers and workers' organizations) and in its own structures and processes;
- promoting gender equality through technical cooperation around the world; and
- promoting gender equality through the management, dissemination and sharing of relevant knowledge.

The ILO has adopted two important instruments for ensuring accountability on gender equality in recent years. They are the most recent Resolution on gender equality, pay equity and maternity protection, adopted at the 2004 International Labour Conference and calling for more active contribution to eliminating gender discrimination and promoting gender equality,[1] and a Decision, taken by the ILO's Governing Body in March 2005, making gender mainstreaming (see p. 92) obligatory in all the ILO's technical cooperation activities. Emphasis on gender equality in technical cooperation was reinforced in the 2006 ILC Resolution and Conclusions on technical cooperation, which says that the ILO should "actively promote mainstreaming of gender equality in donor partnership agreements" (ILO, 2006d, para. 22).

Social dialogue, typifying the ILO's inclusive approach to all its work, also underpins gender equality by recognizing the need for women and men to have an equal voice in the world of work.

3. International labour Conventions and Recommendations

International labour standards are primarily tools for governments which are seeking to draft and implement labour law and social policy, in consultation with employers' and workers' organizations, to acceptable international norms. They prescribe, among other things, minimum working conditions and the principle of non-discrimination in its many aspects, and are usually designed

---

[1] Earlier Resolutions on gender equality were adopted by the ILC in 1975, 1985 and 1991.

for all workers irrespective of their sex, ethnicity, physical ability, or other attributes.

Conventions are international treaties open to ratification by ILO member States. Ratification means that a country undertakes to apply the provisions of the ratified Convention in law and practice, and to submit to regular international supervision on the extent of application. Ratifying countries must provide regular reports to the ILO on the measures taken to implement the Convention, and must accept the ILO's supervision of compliance. If a Convention is not yet ratified by a member State, it represents a goal to be reached. In fact, millions of workers benefit from national laws that are influenced by ILO Conventions even when the country has not (yet) ratified them.

Recommendations set non-binding guidelines to orient national policy and practice which may be used as a source of inspiration or interpretation. They may supplement the provisions contained in a parallel Convention on the same issue.

ILO Conventions and Recommendations are adopted by the annual International Labour Conference. National delegations of government, workers' and employers' representatives meet annually in Geneva to discuss, adopt and supervise standards governing the world of labour.

Countries which have ratified a Convention must implement it. They should repeal any statutory provisions and modify any administrative instructions or procedures that are inconsistent with the Convention. The governments of States which have ratified a Convention report regularly to the Committee of Experts on the Application of Conventions and Recommendations (CEACR) on its application in law and in practice. Workers' and employers' organizations have the right to submit information as well. In countries which have ratified the Tripartite Consultation Convention, 1976 (No. 144), the social partners should all be consulted before government replies, proposals or reports are sent to the CEACR. The report of the CEACR, an independent body, is discussed in the tripartite Committee on the Application of Standards at the International Labour Conference. Shortcomings are pointed out and governments are offered technical assistance to correct them.

Promoting the ratification and proper application of the Conventions and Recommendations is a key activity of the ILO. In particular, the promotion of the key standards for gender equality is a central responsibility of the ILO's Bureau for Gender Equality.

Gender equality in labour standards

Labour standards address gender equality in different ways. Some are gender-explicit, referring specifically to gender equality or non-discrimination, women, or men, e.g. the Conventions on equal remuneration between women and men,

1951 (No. 100), maternity protection, 2000 (No. 183), termination of employment, 1982 (No. 158), and employment policy, 1964 (No. 122). Others are gender-sensitive – standards whose provisions by their nature take into account women's and men's needs but do not mention men and women explicitly, e.g. the Conventions on workers with family responsibilities, 1981 (No. 156), elimination of the worst forms of child labour, 1999 (No. 182), part-time workers, 1994 (No. 175) and home workers, 1996 (No. 177), and a range of standards dealing with working conditions such as safety, security and transport. The fundamental Convention No. 111 spans these two groups, since it addresses discrimination and therefore gender equality but is not exclusively about gender-based discrimination. A third group of Conventions comprises technical standards whose texts are fairly neutral but which may have gender specificities in their application, for instance in the collection and use of statistics. They include areas such as payment of wages, occupational accidents and injuries, hours of work, and social security.

Four ILO Conventions have been designated as key instruments for achieving gender equality in the world of work:

- Equal Remuneration Convention, 1951 (No. 100);
- Discrimination (Employment and Occupation) Convention, 1958 (No. 111);
- Workers with Family Responsibilities Convention, 1981 (No. 156);
- Maternity Protection Convention, 2000 (No. 183).

An important strategy used by the ILO to achieve the global goal of decent work is to promote the ratification and application of the labour standards relevant to equality. The four key equality Conventions are of particular importance, but other Conventions and Recommendations relevant to gender equality, such as those related to employment promotion, working conditions, and migrant workers, are also promoted. It is also important to note that the promotion of standards with obvious gender equality aspects in no way precludes the promotion of equality in the application of standards which are not specifically gender-related.

The Declaration on Fundamental Principles and Rights at Work is also a very important element in the framework for promoting women workers' rights and gender equality (see *Fundamental principles and rights at work*, p. 87).

4. Gender equality, a fundamental human right

Since the 1990s, the concept of a human-rights-based approach to development has gained in importance and offers a normative framework which is very relevant to standards and standard setting. The rights-based approach naturally includes eliminating all forms of discrimination.

The Declaration on Fundamental Principles and Rights at Work and its Follow-up, adopted by the International Labour Conference in 1998, sets out the following areas in which fundamental rights and principles are to be promoted and realized:

(a)   freedom of association and the effective recognition of the right to collective bargaining;

(b)   the elimination of all forms of forced or compulsory labour;

(c)   the abolition of child labour;

(d)   the elimination of discrimination in respect of employment and occupation.

This means that all ILO member States have an obligation, arising from the very fact of their membership, to respect, promote and realize the principles concerning these fundamental rights.

The ILO has designated eight Conventions as embodying these fundamental principles and rights. Two of these have the specific aim of promoting gender equality: Conventions No. 100 and No. 111.

The protection and promotion of equality between women and men are recognized as fundamental concepts in the major international human rights instruments, including the Universal Declaration of Human Rights (1948); the International Covenants on Civil and Political Rights (ICCPR) and on Economic, Social and Cultural Rights (ICESCR) (1966); the Convention on the Elimination of all Forms of Discrimination against Women (CEDAW) (1979) and its Optional Protocol of 1999; the Convention on the Rights of the Child (1989); the International Convention on the Protection of the Rights of all Migrant Workers and Members of their Families (1990); the UN Declaration on the Elimination of Violence against Women (1993); the Beijing Declaration and Platform for Action (1995) and its follow-up; the Millennium Development Goals; and, most recently, the UN Convention on the Rights of Persons with Disabilities, adopted by the Plenary of the General Assembly on 13 December 2006. Such provisions are also binding on States which have not ratified specific ILO instruments but have ratified these more general international standards. Many of the treaty bodies established to monitor compliance with the UN instruments have in their regular reporting paid special attention to gender issues, and indeed have mainstreamed gender equality in their questions to States Parties.

As well as international instruments, national human rights machineries, including commissions for equality and equal opportunities, are valuable instruments for winning and protecting equal rights in the world of work. They exist in many countries. In South Africa, for example, the South African Human Rights Commission (SAHRC), created under section 189 of the Constitution, has successfully taken a high profile especially on discrimination issues. The SAHRC exists alongside a national Commission on Gender Equality, also established by the Constitution (section 187). Some have argued that the parallel existence of these two bodies could result in women's rights being marginalized, and accordingly there have been several efforts to coordinate their work. Carrying that trend further, the United Kingdom's Equality Act of 2006 – the precursor to a promised Single Equality Act aimed at combining all the existing equality enactments (on race, gender, disability, etc.) within Great Britain – has established an overarching Commission for Equality and Human Rights.

5. History of standard setting to promote women workers' rights and gender equality

Discrimination on the grounds of sex is a major form of discrimination, and has been a focus of attention for the international community since the Second World War.

The protection and promotion of women workers' rights have always been integral to the ILO's mandate. The employment of women before and after childbirth was the subject of one of the ILO's first Conventions, dating from 1919, the very first year of the Organization's life. Maternity protection remains a key issue in the promotion of gender equality, as the third Convention on this theme, Convention No. 183, shows. Convention No. 100, by guaranteeing equal pay for work of equal value, opened the door to the examination of structural gender biases in the labour market. Since then there has been a gradual shift in emphasis from protecting women to promoting equality and improving the living and working conditions of workers of either sex on an equal basis, as can be seen, for instance, in the replacement of the Employment (Women with Family Responsibilities) Recommendation, 1965 (No. 123) by the Convention No. 156. In the new millennium, new and revised labour standards reflect the overarching goal of decent work, which now underpins all the ILO's activity. Gender equality is central to this goal.

In the early decades of the twentieth century, women were perceived as more fragile than men, both physically and socially, and therefore as not suited to certain forms of work, particularly any activity which might endanger their health and especially their childbearing function. Minimum standards regarding maternity leave and benefits were consequently among the first instruments adopted by the ILO. In the early 1950s, the emphasis shifted to the promotion of equality between men and women in employment and remuneration. In 1951, Convention No. 100 and its accompanying Recommendation on equal remuneration (No. 90) laid down the guiding principles of equal remuneration for work of equal value regardless of sex. In 1958, Convention No. 111 and the Discrimination (Employment and Occupation) Recommendation (No. 111) were adopted to establish the principle of non-discrimination on a number of grounds including sex, with regard to access to vocational training, access to employment, and terms and conditions of employment. Conventions 100 and 111 are among the most widely ratified of all ILO Conventions[2] and have influenced the drafting of subsequent and related United Nations Conventions and regional instruments.

Other early standards related to occupational safety and health, such as the Lead Poisoning (Women and Children) Recommendation, 1919 (No. 4), the White Phosphorus Recommendation, 1919 (No. 6), and the White Lead (Painting) Convention, 1921 (No. 13), contained specific provisions prohibiting the employment of women in certain areas and for certain processes, reflecting the concern with not endangering women workers' reproductive health. While these instruments (and the Benzene Convention (No. 136) and Recommendation (No. 144) of 1971 are due to be revised, several up to date instruments contain similar women-specific provisions, right up to the very recent Safety and Health in Agriculture Convention (No. 184) and Recommendation (No. 192) of 2001. Convention No. 89 prohibiting night work for women in industry, adopted in 1948 (following the earlier Night Work (Women) Convention, 1919 (No. 4) and Night Work (Women) Convention (Revised), 1934 (No. 41)), was made more flexible through the Protocol of 1990, and a new Night Work Convention (No. 171) and Recommendation (No. 178) were adopted in 1990, now protecting both men and women against the hazardous effects of night work. However, women-specific provisions are still the subject of debate, for a large number of ILO member States consider them discriminatory.

From the 1960s, standards promoting equality were increasingly based on the recognition that equality implies the sharing of family responsibilities between men and women. As women gained a growing share of the labour market – though not always in full-time jobs – the male breadwinner in full-time work came to represent the model of the "typical" worker less and less. Labour standards began to reflect this shift in 1965, when Recommendation No. 123 on women with family responsibilities was adopted, covering measures that should be taken to enable women workers to fulfil their various responsibilities harmoniously and without discrimination. From the early 1980s, as the focus of analysis concerning equality in general was reoriented from women to relations between women and men (see *Gender analysis and planning*, p. 90), the conviction gained ground that any change in the role of women should be

---

[2] As of 17 Feb. 2007, Convention No. 100 has 163 ratifications and Convention No. 111, 165. For more information, see: http://www.ilo.org/ilolex/english/docs/declworld.htm.

accompanied by a change in that of men and should be reflected in their greater participation in family and household duties. In accordance with this thinking, Convention No. 156 and its accompanying Recommendation No. 165 concerning workers with family responsibilities were adopted in 1981. These instruments apply to men as well as women with responsibilities for dependent children or other members of their immediate family, and are intended to facilitate their employment without discrimination resulting from such family responsibilities.

A number of standards adopted more recently respond to the rapid changes in the labour market and in modalities of work in the face of growing globalization from the 1980s onward. For example, Convention No. 175 and Recommendation No. 182 of 1994, aiming at the equal treatment of full- and part-time workers, are important for gender equality because most part-time workers are women. The Convention No. 177 and Recommendation No. 184 concerning home work, adopted in 1996, contribute to improving the situation of millions of homeworkers, a large majority of whom are women. Convention No. 182 and Recommendation No. 190, aiming at the prohibition and elimination of the worst forms of child labour, also have a gender component, calling for account to be taken of the special situation of girls. Convention No. 183 is one of the ILO's four key equality Conventions, as noted above.

The Maritime Labour Convention, 2006 is coherent with Conventions Nos. 100 and 111 as regards discrimination in general and equal pay for work of equal value in particular; it also enjoins upon member States the provision of equal welfare facilities for seafarers irrespective of sex or other attributes. Several recent Recommendations contain clauses referring to the importance of observing and promoting gender equality; they include the Promotion of Cooperatives Recommendation, 2002 (No. 193); the Human Resources Development Recommendation, 2004 (No. 195); and Employment Relationship, 2006 (No. 198). The last of these aims to encourage member States to adopt national policies regulating the employment relationship, particularly in the case of "vulnerable workers", including women workers. This is of particular importance to women workers in atypical and highly feminized types of work.

6. Sources of gender equality law: International labour standards, supranational law and national law

This guide focuses on women workers' and gender equality rights derived from international law, i.e. the corpus of internationally-agreed instruments consisting of the ILO's own Conventions and Recommendations and other relevant instruments such as those mentioned above. International labour standards may describe general principles such as equal pay, equal opportunity and treatment between men and women, and are designed as minimum standards. Individual countries may go further and provide a higher level of protection, such as a longer period of maternity leave, or other more favourable provisions. The law applicable in an individual case might therefore derive from international and from national law.

In addition, supranational law might be relevant. The European Community has adopted a number of directives concerning equal pay, equal treatment of women and men at the workplace, statutory social security, occupational pension schemes, maternity protection, parental leave, part-time work and the burden of proof in sex discrimination cases. European equality law ranks higher than national law and is valid throughout the member States of the European Union (EU). The same applies to a large number of rulings of the European Court of Justice in the field of equality between men and women. There is thus an interplay between the law on equality at three different levels.

Other regional or subregional initiatives, apart from legally binding instruments, may influence legal development at national levels. In the Caribbean, for instance, the Caribbean Community (CARICOM) has adopted, as part of its project on labour legislation harmonization, model legislation on equal opportunities and treatment for women and men in employment, as a guide for legislation in member States. In South Asia, the South Asian Association for Regional Cooperation (SAARC) Convention on Preventing and Combating the Trafficking in Women and Children for Prostitution was signed in 2002 (SAARC, 2002). The Commonwealth countries drew up the Victoria Falls Declaration of Principles for Promoting the Human Rights of Women in 1994, and it has been followed up by further instruments. The Belém do Pará Convention, adopted by the Organization of American States in 1994, deals with the prevention, punishment and eradication of violence against women, as does the 1998 Addendum to the Southern African Development Community's 1997 Declaration on Gender and Development.

7. Application and enforcement at the national level

Gender mainstreaming in the application of international labour standards is important because it helps to ensure that women and men have equal access to benefits derived from those standards. It accords equal recognition to the needs, experiences and interests of women and men when they are different as well as when they are the same. Government reports submitted to the ILO under articles 19 and 22 of the ILO Constitution, which provide the framework for member States' regular reporting procedures, refer to cases of discrimination in employment based on a number of grounds not mentioned in Convention No. 111, including marital status, sexual orientation and HIV status. The ILO also has constitutional procedures for address disputes related to member States' compliance with standards under ratified Conventions.

Many countries have adopted specific legislation prohibiting discrimination and promoting equality in employment, and many national constitutions contain clauses specifying such equality. The more recent emphasis is on governments' positive duty to prevent discrimination and promote equality. But the law is not consistently applied and inequality persists. Now, emphasis is increasingly placed on enforcement through legal, administrative and promotional measures to fill the continuing gaps between the law and its application, using specific institutions.

Women workers often encounter de facto disadvantages as a result of apparently "neutral" provisions in laws or collective agreements. These might imply a case of indirect discrimination. Discrimination may be "direct" – making a *distinctive* difference between the sexes – or *apparently neutral,* but in fact producing inequality and therefore constituting "indirect" discrimination. Both manifestations of discrimination fall under the scope of the relevant Conventions. The distinction is important because whereas forms of direct discrimination seem to be declining, cases of indirect discrimination, which are more difficult to detect or to prove, appear to be on the increase. In addition, there is institutional discrimination, which emerges from labour market forces or structural inequalities in employment and occupation.

In most countries, equality legislation in the form of labour codes, equal opportunities laws or general employment statutes, is supervised by the labour inspectorate. This verifies through the inspection of premises and records that the enterprises under examination comply with the requirements of the law. Modern labour inspection services are perceived less and less to be "workplace police", and see their role nowadays as providing information and advice for employers and workers on the most effective means of complying with the legal provisions. Labour inspectors may have the power to refer a complaint to the appropriate authorities or initiate proceedings before the courts or tribunals.

As part of the framework of national machinery to improve the status of women and promote equality, a number of countries and supranational bodies have established human rights and/or equality commissions which may examine complaints of discrimination and monitor the implementation of anti-discrimination measures (see section 4, p. 6). These agencies can facilitate the filing and resolution of individual or collective actions. In some countries, the filing of a claim with an Equal Opportunities Commission is a procedural prerequisite to pursuing any employment discrimination complaint.

Depending on the national system, international as well as national standards may have to be observed by the labour courts or other competent bodies. Once international law is transformed into national law or is given effect through collective bargaining, the respective national provision is usually referred to.

In general, over the past decade, labour court judges, lawyers and others involved in litigation procedures have become more aware of the implications of sex discrimination. Some key cases have demonstrated the importance of judicial advancement of workplace equality. There is, however, criticism – and also some evidence – that legal systems dominated by men who do not understand the equality issue may constitute an obstacle to the enforcement process. To facilitate litigation in cases of sex discrimination, legal aid, a modification of the burden of proof (see *Burden of proof*, p. 24), and protection against reprisal are useful tools.

8. ILO standard setting and other means of action

International labour Conventions and Recommendations play an important role in promoting equality because they represent an international and tripartite consensus on minimum standards. While these standards generally apply to both men and women workers, a number of them specifically address rights referring to women workers and gender equality, and these should be respected and pursued in all ILO programmes. As already mentioned, these standards deal with equal remuneration, equality of opportunity and treatment between men and women in employment, maternity protection, workers with family responsibilities, and part-time and home work.

The concept of equality in employment does not imply that men and women are identical (see *Gender equality*, p. 91) or that their roles or needs are identical. Indeed the concept of equality, and even more that of gender equity seek to give equal value and recognition to the different natures, roles and needs of women and men. The roles and positions of men and women differ to a great extent in any society and are conditioned by historical perspective as well as the current situation. Their respective needs may vary accordingly. In most, if not all, societies, women have to fulfil specific roles as mothers, homemakers and providers of basic needs. This usually implies that they have a weaker position as regards access to jobs and training, equal pay, rights to land and other capital assets, and freedom of movement. To generate progress towards gender equity, these existing imbalances need to be addressed in the design of policies, programmes and projects.

Standard setting and technical cooperation are important and complementary ways in which the ILO contributes to attaining social justice and decent work.

International labour standards define the goals, means and approaches in social policy, whereas technical cooperation helps achieve social progress in practical terms. Technical cooperation, at the request of ILO member States, is therefore linked with the promotion of international labour standards and human rights in a comprehensive and complementary approach.

Both standard setting and technical cooperation must be based on systematic research and documentation. Thus the ILO is involved in numerous research programmes, research networks and advocacy, and in compiling and analysing data on gender-related issues. This information is made available to ILO constituents and the public through publications, electronic databases, meetings, seminars and workshops.

Advisory services and capacity building for constituents are other key means of action through which the ILO promotes equality between men and women in the world of work.

A

Access to employment

Equal opportunities for access to employment must be guaranteed, to workers of both sexes, before and during the hiring process. Employment agencies, both public and private, should promote equal employment opportunities by:

*   encouraging applications from all eligible workers, men and women, and reviewing the recruitment records for both sexes;

*   rejecting discriminatory requests from prospective employers, and informing them of the law and national policies on equal opportunities;

*   informing applicants of their right to equal employment opportunities;

*   Informing applicants of any policies and practices concerning work–family reconciliation measures.

According to the Convention No. 183, pregnancy or motherhood should not constitute a source of discrimination in access to employment, and member States should take appropriate measures to ensure this. Tests for pregnancy or certification of non-pregnancy should not be required of a woman applying for employment, except where national laws or regulations restrict the employment of pregnant or nursing women in specific situations, for instance work deemed hazardous to the mother or the child. Similarly, known or suspected HIV-positive status should not be the sole grounds for refusing a job to an applicant of either sex, unless it can be objectively established in good faith that seronegativity is a necessary occupational requirement.

As regards access to employment for workers with family responsibilities, Convention No. 156 calls for the right to engage in employment without discrimination, free choice of employment, and training and guidance to promote access to employment for such workers. Recommendation No. 165 expands on these principles.

Small and micro-enterprises in a variety of economic sectors are important sources of employment and self-employment for women in both developed and developing countries, and there has been a significant rise in the number of women entrepreneurs. Small and medium-sized enterprises offer a good channel of access to employment for women; but policy, regulatory and institutional environments are frequently unfriendly to women and/or small enterprises and women's access to credit, technology, assets such as land or premises and training is often lower than that for men. Access to employment of this kind can be promoted by means of specific measures and incentives for women aspiring to become entrepreneurs.

> *C. 111 and R. 111: Discrimination (Employment and Occupation), 1958*
> *C. 122: Employment Policy, 1964*
> *R. 169: Employment Policy (Supplementary Provisions), 1984*
> *C. 88: Employment Service, 1948*
> *C. 142: Human Resources Development, 1975*
> *C. 156 and R. 165: Workers with Family Responsibilities, 1981*
> *R. 189: Job Creation in Small and Medium-sized Enterprises, 1998*
> *C. 181 and R. 188: Private Employment Agencies, 1997*
> *C. 183: Maternity Protection, 2000*
> *R. 103: Promotion of Cooperatives, 2002*
> *R. 195: Human Resources Development, 2004*

➡ See also **Advertising for workers; Cooperatives; Family responsibilities, workers with; Selection procedures; Women's entrepreneurship; Work–family balance**

Accidents

➡ See **Occupational safety and health**; see also **Employment injury benefit; Labour inspection; Mines**

Advertising for workers

Advertising should not indicate any preference for applicants of one sex or any other particular personal attribute unless the preference is clearly justified as job-related and necessary. The following are some general guidelines to gender-aware job advertisement:

- Illustrations which suggest that the job is only for men or for women should be avoided.

- Applications from both women and men should be encouraged, for example by using wording such as "applications from women as well as men are welcomed". In specific sectors or professions where one sex is under-represented, wording encouraging members of the under-represented sex to apply may be helpful.

• Advertisements should state that the employing entity is an equal opportunities employer.

• Advertisements should not contain irrelevant job requirements which could limit women's applications.

• Selection criteria should be objective, related to the requirements of the job and consistently applied to all applicants; criteria such as sex, age, appearance and physical characteristics should not influence selection.

• Advertisements should reach the widest range of potential applicants; they should, for instance, be distributed where potential applicants of either sex gather or will hear about the job.

• Qualifications required should be based on a current job description which accurately identifies the purpose and function of the job.

C. 111 and R. 111: Discrimination (Employment and Occupation), 1958
C. 181 and R. 188: Private Employment Agencies, 1997

➜ See also **Access to employment; Labour administration; Public employment services and private employment agencies**

Affirmative action

Affirmative action – also termed positive measures – to counter sex discrimination comprises special, usually temporary, measures to redress the effects of past or continuing discrimination in order to establish de facto equality of opportunity and treatment between men and women. Such measures are targeted at a particular group and are intended to eliminate and prevent discrimination and to offset disadvantages arising from existing attitudes, behaviour and structures based on stereotypes concerning the division of social roles between men and women. The adoption of positive measures stems from the observation that the legal banning of discrimination has not proved sufficient in itself to create equity in the world of work. Affirmative actions are necessary to put everyone on an equal footing, especially where historically entrenched socio-economic inequalities arise out of a history of oppression of one group by another. Article 5.2 of Convention No. 111 lists legitimate grounds for special measures designed to meet particular requirements. Such measures are deemed not to be discriminatory but to constitute affirmative action (ILO, 1996, ch. 3).

Affirmative action in favour of women should not be considered as discriminatory against men in a transitional period. Once the consequences of past discrimination have been rectified, the measures should be removed or adjusted so as to prevent discrimination against men. To avoid unintended backlash, it is advisable to undertake consultation with all stakeholders before instituting positive measures (see *Social dialogue*, p. 171).

Affirmative action for women may encompass a wide range of measures, including corrective action such as:

- setting targets, goals or quotas for women's participation in activities or sectors, or at levels from which they have previously been excluded and in which they are still under-represented;

- promoting women's access to wider opportunities in education, vocational training and employment in non-traditional sectors and at higher levels of responsibility;

- placement, guidance and counselling services, provision for gender-trained personnel familiar with the special needs of employed and unemployed women;

- fast-track career measures, including mentoring and pairing within existing networks;

- informing and motivating employers to recruit and promote women, especially in the sectors and categories mentioned;

- eliminating stereotypes;

- promoting the active participation of women in decision-making bodies within and beyond the world of work;

- adapting working conditions and adjusting work organization to suit the needs of workers with family responsibilities;

- adopting contract compliance policies within the framework of public spending;[3]

- fostering greater sharing of occupational, family and social responsibilities between men and women.

Affirmative action may be more effective when it is developed and applied through cooperation between the government, and the employers and trade unions concerned; when it suits the needs and possibilities of the employees and employers; and when it is effectively monitored and followed up with

---

[3] See, for example, http://www.ilo.org/public/english/employment/gems/eeo/law/usa/i_ofccp.htm, on the US Office of Federal Contract Compliance Programs.

adequate government resources. The government should play a leading role in implementing such programmes for public sector employment.

Public service commissions are potentially useful as an instrument for actively promoting equality of opportunity as regards both gender and other aspects of diversity.

Affirmative action should also involve the recognition that in certain circumstances men may also suffer discrimination. Affirmative action in favour of men might also be a way to increase the number of men working in female-dominated occupations. In some transitional economies, it is becoming recognized that there is a need to address the special needs of men who have been lost their jobs in state-owned enterprises and have withdrawn from economic activity in discouragement.

> *C. 111 and R. 111: Discrimination (Employment and Occupation), 1958*
> *C. 156 and R. 165: Workers with Family Responsibilities, 1981*
> *C. 159 and R. 168: Vocational Rehabilitation and Employment*
> *(Disabled Persons), 1983*
> *C. 169: Indigenous and Tribal Peoples, 1989*
> *R. 193: Promotion of Cooperatives, 2002*
> *R. 195: Human Resources Development, 2004*

➜ See also **Employment policy and promotion; Job description; Non-traditional occupations; Occupational segregation; Social dialogue; Vocational guidance; Vocational training**

Agricultural and other rural workers

More people in the world still work in agriculture than in any other sector of the world economy – 40 per cent in 2005 (ILO, 2006a, p. 25). A majority of the world's women workers are still concentrated in rural areas, occupied mostly in farming, but increasingly also in rural non-farming activities. In economies in which agriculture is a major economic sector, women work more often in this sector than men (ILO, 2004a, p. 25). Women's participation rates in these sectors are often higher than in most other sectors, but this is simply a reflection of the way work is organized in these sectors, where there is a high proportion of family-owned small farms and non-farm units. Women represent a higher share than men of agricultural workers and unpaid workers on household farms; when men migrate to the city for jobs, for instance, women are left behind to tend the farm. Women agricultural workers in many are countries in a particularly powerless position, since they cannot own or inherit land and thus cannot participate in benefits for which land ownership is a prerequisite, such as membership of cooperatives, credit unions or agricultural extension programmes.

While all rural workers endure long hours, low incomes, and exposure to occupational safety and health hazards, women often bear the brunt of these conditions because of their greater concentration in occasional and seasonal work. In order to provide some protection against such adverse conditions, international labour standards on the right to freedom of association in agriculture, adopted as early as 1921 and in 1975, covered all rural workers defined as persons engaged in agriculture, handicrafts or related occupations in rural areas. In 2001 new standards on occupational safety and health in agriculture (Convention No. 184 and Recommendation No. 192) were adopted. They cover health protection by monitoring pregnant and nursing mothers, young workers and older workers (R. 192, II.4 (3)). Article 18 of Convention No. 184 also provides that "measures shall be taken to ensure that the special needs of women agricultural workers are taken into account in relation to pregnancy, breastfeeding and reproductive health".

In practice, the prevalence of family-owned or own-account farms, combined with low literacy rates, language barriers and ignorance of workers' rights, has impeded the spread of trade unions in rural areas, except to some extent in plantations and agribusiness sectors. This applies specifically to women because their literacy rate is lower than that of men. Women working in agriculture are often not recognized as basic producers by rural extension services that mainly address men, and support services such as rural training and credit are difficult for women to access sometimes because rural women do not speak the official language of the country or cannot read. Consequently, women have little negotiating power and are often denied even basic workers' rights. Women working in rural areas should be entitled to the same employment conditions as those working in other sectors.

Forced labour through debt bondage is prevalent in rural societies in a number of countries, particularly in South Asia. Indirect bondage, in which women and children are bonded through the male household head, is characteristic of the agriculture sector. Women may be "traded" as part of the man's debt and are often expected to do housework for the landlord as well as farm labour. Some South Asian countries, notably Pakistan, are becoming increasingly committed to tackling bonded labour both in farms and industries.

> *C. 11: Right of Association (Agriculture), 1921*
>
> *C. 129: Labour Inspection (Agriculture), 1969*
>
> *C. 141 and R. 149: Rural Workers' Organisations, 1975*
>
> *C. 184 and R. 192: Safety and Health in Agriculture, 2001*

➜ See also **Child labour; Forced labour; Freedom of association and the right to organize; Occupational safety and health; Plantation workers**

Atypical work

The category atypical work (also known as non-standard work) covers a large and growing variety of forms of work and employment characterized by flexibility (see Flexibility of labour, p. __) and reduced security. They include part-time work, casual and seasonal work, job sharing, fixed-term contracts, temporary agency work, home-based work, Remote working; self-employment, and the work of unpaid spouses or family members in small family-run enterprises. These forms of work differ from the norm historically regarded as "typical" or standard, namely full-time, socially secure employment of unlimited duration, with a single employer, performed at the employer's workplace and with a guaranteed regular income. In fact, the proliferation of atypical work is such that it is becoming less and less possible to describe permanent, full-time jobs as the norm, and more and more important to address the issues of access to employment, decent working conditions, adequate social protection, and opportunities to organize and exercise voice among all kinds of "atypical" workers.

Much atypical work is informal and poorly, or not at all, covered by social security systems. However, the regulation of atypical work confronts a double challenge: the lack of regulation per se and the inability of traditional labour laws to extend effectively to atypical work (for example, in the case of rights that require a qualifying period which do not extend to many temporary workers).[4] The current legal trend is toward recognizing the rights of atypical or non-standard workers through (a) the specific regulation of non-standard work by extending and revising existing protections, and (b) introducing rights to equal treatment for atypical workers. Convention No. 183 is a recent example (see Article 2 of the Convention)

Whereas men are over-represented in "typical" or "standard" employment relationships, women have always been over-represented in atypical forms of work, especially as part-time or casual workers. Women's massive incorporation into atypical work in the globalized economy has both positive and negative aspects. On the one hand, it has improved the social and economic status of a great many women through waged employment and has made it easier for them to combine work outside the home with housework and family responsibilities. On the other hand, the kinds of work available are often low-status, low-paid and with poor working conditions; the lack of regulation of atypical work militates against job security and social protection. Women workers also predominate in occupations and sectors where there is a high incidence of disguised or unclear employment relationships.

---

[4] A qualifying period is a period that must be worked before a legal right becomes available to individual workers; the right to protection from unfair dismissal, for instance, is commonly subject to a year's qualifying period.

C. 183 and R. 191: Maternity Protection, 2000

→ See also **Casual work; Employment relationship; Flexibility of labour; Globalization; Home work; Informal economy; Labour force; Labour market; Labour statistics; Precarious work; Remote working; Social protection; Unemployment**

B

Benzene

→ See **Chemicals**

Biological risks

Biological risks arise from exposure to, or handling of, toxic, infectious or aller-genic biological agents and waste. As with chemicals, some substances of this kind are particularly harmful to pregnant and nursing mothers and young people. Maternity Protection Recommendation, 2000 (No. 191) specifically states (Paragraph 6 (3) (b)) that measures should be taken to find alternative work for pregnant or nursing workers if their jobs involve exposure to biological, chemical or physical agents which represent a reproductive health hazard. More generally and without specific reference to any population group, several standards refer to the need for protection against biological risks (for example, see Recommendation No. 192, Paragraph 8).

> *C. 155: Occupational Safety and Health, 1981*
> *R. 171: Occupational Health Services, 1985*
> *C. 167 and R175: Safety and Health in Construction, 1988*
> *C. 176: Safety and Health in Mines, 1995*
> *R. 191: Maternity Protection, 2000*
> *C. 184 and R. 192: Safety and Health in Agriculture, 2001*
> *R. 194: List of Occupational Diseases, 2002*
> *MLC: Maritime Labour Convention, 2006*

→ See also **Chemicals; Hygiene in the workplace; Maternity protection; Occupational safety and health**

Bonded labour

→ See **Forced labour**

Breastfeeding workers

According to Article 3 of Convention No. 183, member States

> shall, after consulting the representative organizations of employers and workers, adopt appropriate measures to ensure that pregnant or breastfeeding women are not obliged to perform work which has been determined by the competent authority to be prejudicial to the health of the mother or the child, or where an assessment has established a significant risk to the mother's health or that of her child.

The Convention and its accompanying Recommendation (No. 191) also stipulate that the breastfeeding worker should be provided with the right to one or more daily breaks or a daily reduction of hours of work to breastfeed her child. She should have the right to interrupt her work for this purpose, and such interruptions or reductions in daily hours of work should be counted as working time and remunerated accordingly. While the first Maternity Protection Convention, 1919 (No. 3), specified two half-hour nursing breaks and the Maternity Protection Recommendation, 1952 (No. 95), called for one and a half hours per day, the current Convention leaves it to national law and practice to determine the matter of determining the period during which nursing breaks or the reduction of daily hours of work are allowed, the number and duration of nursing breaks, and procedures for the reduction of daily hours of work. Adjustments to meet special needs are permitted on the basis of a medical certificate.

Where practicable, provision should be made for the establishment of facilities for nursing under adequate hygienic conditions at or near the workplace.

> *C. 103: Maternity Protection (Revised) and R95: Maternity Protection, 1952*
> *C. 183 and R. 191: Maternity Protection, 2000*

→   See also **Hours of work; Maternity protection**

Bullying

→   See **Harassment and pressure**

Burden of proof

The burden of proof is a legal procedural rule which has important consequences if an assertion is not proven. Normally, if a person files a legal complaint before a civil or labour court, it is up to her or him to prove the facts corresponding to the alleged claim. If the burden of proof is not met by the complainant, the opposing party does not need to defend the claim.

However, the nature of discrimination cases often makes proof difficult if not impossible because perceptions of discrimination are inevitably subjective, the complainant often has little or no information on the employer's internal policies and procedures, and the actual rationale of a workplace measure or action may not be revealed.

It is generally national legislation that determines the levels of proof required and whether the burden should be heavy (for example beyond reasonable doubt) or may be lighter (for example more probable than not). In order to facilitate the legal pursuit of rights for victims of discrimination, a growing number of national legal systems and the supranational EU have modified this general rule in favour of the complainant: the burden of proof remains, in principle, on the party who claims to be discriminated against, but allegations must be substantiated only to a lower level of probability. If the complainant is able to show some evidence pointing to discrimination (a "prima facie case"), the burden of proof moves to the employer, who must either rebut this evidence or produce contrary evidence ("shifting" or "reversing" the burden of proof). The respective provisions are based on the fact that it is usually the employer who is in an advantageous position and in possession of all the documents or other relevant evidence and that if there is indeed a valid reason for the prejudicial treatment, this should not be difficult to prove.

Shifting or reversing the burden of proof improves the chances for victims of discrimination to win their cases and may therefore be an effective means of combating unequal pay or treatment at the workplace.

> *C. 158: Termination of Employment, 1982*
> *R. 198: Employment Relationship, 2006*

➤ See also **Discrimination; Dismissal; Equal remuneration**

C

Call centres

➜ See **Remote working**

Care work

Care work may be very broadly defined as the work of looking after the physical, psychological, emotional and developmental needs of one or more other people. Care recipients are generally identified as infants, school-age children, people who are ill, persons with a disability, and elderly people. Care providers typically include public and private health services, state-regulated or public-sector social workers, public or private care-provider agencies, enterprises of employment, voluntary and community organizations, faith-based organizations or networks, and relatives and friends. Different settings and modalities of care work apply to each of these categories.

However, care work is difficult to conceptualize for policy-making and regulatory purposes. It is done visibly, as formal employment in institutions, and invisibly and informally, in the home (one's own or someone else's). It is sometimes remunerated and sometimes not. It varies widely in intensity and effort: it may involve little more than watching and monitoring, or it may mean almost constant physical and emotional attention to a person in intimate and stressful circumstances and involving serious responsibilities of a paramedical nature. The emotional input it demands is much greater than in many other forms of work. All this makes it hard for politicians and statisticians to arrive at a clear and workable definition of care work (Daly, 2001, pp. 16–18).

It is now generally recognized that care work is real work, whatever the setting in which it is performed. However, this recognition is only very recent and was brought about under opposing pressures from orthodox economists and politicians seeking to reduce care's financial burden on the state on the one hand, and from feminists seeking to make care visible and countable on the other. Yet people who provide care for other people often do not see themselves as workers in the traditional sense of the term even where there is financial remuneration.

Very often there is no remuneration, yet this unpaid work has also begun to be recognized. In 2006, the ILO expressly recognized as work "the unpaid work in the family and community that is often ignored in current thinking about the economy and society ... much of this work is done by women and is essential to the welfare not just of the young or elderly or sick but also to those in paid work. It is also often carried out alongside paid work." (ILO, 2006a, p. vi).

Care work is also an extreme manifestation of both horizontal and vertical occupational segregation by sex. Women continue to be mainly responsible for the "care economy" as an extension, or an integral part, of domestic labour. Care work has low status and attracts low pay if performed as employment and none at all when performed as housework.

Care work will inevitably become more important because of changes in demographic patterns and in the nature of the family, changes in the social and economic status of women, and changes in welfare states. The notions of both care as work and the need for care, already fluid, are very likely to evolve further and become broader. Both carers and recipients of care have rights; therefore both the rights and the responsibilities of carers need to be regulated. A collective voice capable of bargaining and advocating for care providers particularly outside a commercial relationship, is essential. At present however, the diversity of care work, spanning the public and private spheres and a huge variety of settings and tasks, makes any unified representation and voice for all care workers difficult to achieve.

The State should have four functions in the regulation of care work:

- establishing an appropriate regulatory framework, consisting of laws and regulations setting standards of acceptable behaviour by individual providers and recipients, and standards and rules for institutions and agencies directly involved in providing and managing care;

- deciding on what, if any, income transfers should be provided, and to whom;

- establishing a system for monitoring, evaluation and penalization;

- creating institutions for supplementary care, appropriate to the socio-economic structure (for example encouraging provision of communal facilities in a village or facilities at or near workplaces in enterprises) (Daly, 2001, p. 22).

To date, the only ILO standard to deal specifically with care workers are the Nursing Personnel Convention (No. 149) and its accompanying Recommendation (No. 157) of 1977. ILO standards that are applicable to other categories of workers also apply to care workers, especially as regards equality of opportunity, treatment and remuneration, the right to organize and collective bargaining, and minimum age. As noted above, however, these rights are difficult to obtain in practice owing to the fragmentation of the sector as well as to discriminatory attitudes.

C. 149 and R. 157: Nursing Personnel, 1977

→ See also **Domestic workers; Family responsibilities, workers with; Home work; Housework; Illness in the family, leave for; Informal economy; Nursing personnel; Older women workers; Parental leave**

Career breaks

Career breaks are an important mechanism for enabling reconciliation of work and family life. As regards career breaks related to maternity, Convention No 183 provides for employment security, prohibiting dismissal during pregnancy, maternity leave and a period of time after return to work, and gives the right to reinstatement in the same job or an equivalent one with the same pay (Art. 8).

Article 7 of Convention No. 156 also addresses this issue, stating:

> All measures compatible with national conditions and possibilities, including measures in the field of vocational guidance and training, shall be taken to enable workers with family responsibilities to become and remain integrated in the labour force, as well as to re-enter the labour force after an absence due to those responsibilities.

Recommendation No. 165 (III.12-14) provides that in accordance with national policy and practice, vocational training facilities and, where possible, paid educational leave arrangements should be made available to enable workers with family responsibilities to re-enter employment. Other recommended facilities for such workers include vocational guidance, counselling, information and placement services staffed by suitably trained personnel and capable of responding adequately to the special needs of workers with family responsibilities.

Some countries, such as Belgium, have introduced more far-reaching career-break schemes in which the absence or reduction in working time is not necessarily for the purposes of childbirth or family commitments (European Commission, 2005).

C. 156 and R. 165: Workers with Family Responsibilities, 1981
C. 183 and R. 191: Maternity Protection, 2000

→ See **Family responsibilities, workers with; Paid educational leave; Vocational guidance; Vocational training; Work–family balance; Work–life balance**

Career opportunities

All employees, irrespective of their sex, should be informed equally about promotion, mobility and training opportunities and equally encouraged to pursue suitable opportunities. It should specifically be ensured that:

- all employees are informed of forthcoming vacant positions in a systematic and equitable manner;

- application requirements and procedures for mobility, promotions and training programmes are clearly defined and followed, and information on them is made available to all employees;

- restrictions deriving from agreements or arrangements of custom and practice are removed when they operate to exclude workers of one sex from promotion, transfer and training opportunities, or affect them disproportionately;

- a career progression plan is introduced whereby all job promotion opportunities are made known to encourage the participation of all employees, particularly those who have traditionally been excluded from career progression;

- training and mobility opportunities are available to all employees to avoid occupational segregation in the workplace;

- training programmes are developed and regularly reviewed to assist all employees, in particular women, in overcoming obstacles to their development in employment, specifically in adjusting to structural change and technological innovation, with a view to increasing management and other skills;

- efforts are made to reduce inequalities in participation in training.

Informal means of promoting women's career chances, such as mentoring, may also be provided.

Convention No. 156 on workers with family responsibilities deals with the measures that are to be taken to enable workers with family responsibilities to enter the labour force or re-enter it after a period of absence (Art. 7, see above, Career breaks). Such measures may include vocational training, paid education leave, and a range of information and advisory services suited to the needs of workers with family responsibilities (Recommendation No. 165, Paragraphs 13–14).

> *C. 88 and R. 83: Employment Service, 1948*
> *C. 111 and R. 111: Discrimination (Employment and Occupation), 1958*
> *C. 122 and R. 122: Employment Policy, 1964*

C. 142: Human Resources Development, 1975
C. 156 and R. 165: Workers with Family Responsibilities, 1981
R. 169: Employment Policy (Supplementary Provisions), 1984
R. 195: Human Resources Development, 2004

➔ *See also* **Affirmative action; Career breaks; Family responsibilities, workers with; Human resources development; Paid educational leave; Vocational guidance; Vocational training**

Cash and medical benefits for maternity

The Convention No. 183, which revised Convention No. 103 of 1952, provides that while a woman is away from work on maternity leave she is entitled to cash benefits at a level which ensures that she can maintain herself and her child in proper conditions of health and to a suitable standard of living. She is also entitled to medical benefits, including prenatal, childbirth and postnatal care, as well as hospital care when necessary. According to the Convention (No. 103), it should be possible for her to choose a doctor freely, and also to choose between a public and a private hospital.

Cash benefits are to be provided either by means of compulsory social insurance or from public funds. When cash benefits are provided through compulsory social insurance schemes and are based on earnings, they should not be less than two-thirds of the woman's previous earnings or such of those earnings as are taken into account for computing benefits (C. 183, Art. 6 (3)). Recommendation No. 191 provides that where practicable and after consultation with the representative organizations of employers and workers, these benefits should be raised to the full amount of the woman's previous earnings or the proportion taken into account for benefit computation purposes. The employer should not be individually liable for the cost of these benefits.

C. 102: Social Security (Minimum Standards), 1952
C. 103: Maternity Protection (Revised) and R95: Maternity Protection, 1952
C. 110: Plantations, 1958 (and Protocol, 1982)
C. 165: Social Security (Seafarers) (Revised), 1987
C. 181: Private Employment Agencies, 1997
C. 183 and R. 191: Maternity Protection, 2000

➔ See also **Health during maternity; Maternity leave, Maternity protection; Radiation protection**

Casual work

Casual work is work without a fixed duration performed by workers who are called on to work only as and when they are needed by the employer. They may work full- or part-time for periods of varying duration. Casual work is closely dependent on the level of, and fluctuation in, the workload, and casual workers may work for only a few days or for as long as several weeks in a row. The employment contracts of casual workers – where these exist – can stipulate their minimum and maximum hours of work and the notice period that has to be respected for requiring that they work. Under "zero hours" contracts, however, workers are not entitled to any minimum number of hours of work, but are required to be available to the employer without any assurance that they will be called upon to work (ILO, 2004c).

Casual workers differ from other non-permanent workers in that they may often possess fewer rights and less protection. The absence of a continuing stable relationship with any employer can lead to casual workers not being considered employees at all, even where there is a contract. In other cases, they may lose out on labour rights where these are attached to a qualifying period of employment, which is usually longer than the casual worker's period of work. Casual workers' legal and contractual entitlements are usually limited or absent. For instance, casual workers may be excluded from the terms of the Termination of Employment Convention, 1982 (No. 158), according to the decision of individual member states, by virtue of opt-out clauses open to member States after consultations with the social partners. Article 1 (3) of Convention No. 158 does, however, prohibit the continuous use of short-term contracts aimed at avoiding an employer's obligation to give certain rights to workers.

Many temporary workers can be considered to be casual workers. Although some temporary workers, particularly those who work for private employment agencies, may have longer fixed-term contracts, temporary workers generally receive low wages and have a lower quality of employment.

Casual work, and particularly seasonal casual work, is done by people of both sexes and all ages including many children; but, as with many other forms of precarious work, women predominate in it. In agricultural work, women and children often accompany the male head of household as unpaid family helpers.

Paragraph 2 (a) of Recommendation No. 131 on Invalidity, Old-Age and Survivors' Benefits recommends the gradual extension of invalidity and old-age benefits to persons whose employment is casual.

Under the terms of the Labour Inspection (Agriculture) Convention, 1969 (No. 129), casual or seasonal agricultural workers are implicitly covered under the concept of "employee", thus according them the same right to benefit from labour inspection as permanent full-time workers. Convention No. 169, concerning the rights of indigenous and tribal peoples, refers to casual workers in Article 20.3:

> The measures taken shall include measures to ensure: (a) that workers belonging to the peoples concerned, including seasonal, casual and migrant workers in agricultural and other employment, as well as those employed by labour contractors, enjoy the protection afforded by national law and practice to other such workers in the same sectors, and that they are fully informed of their rights under labour legislation and of the means of redress available to them.

Recommendation No. 165 on workers with family responsibilities, while not mentioning casual workers explicitly, also addresses temporary workers and homeworkers, many of whom have family responsibilities, stating that their terms and conditions of employment, including social security coverage, should be as far as possible equivalent (pro rata) to those of full-time, permanent workers respectively (Paragraph 21 (2)).

> *R. 131: Invalidity, Old-Age and Survivors' Benefits, 1967*
> *C. 129 and R. 133: Labour Inspection (Agriculture), 1969*
> *R. 165: Workers with Family Responsibilities, 1981*
> *C. 169: Indigenous and Tribal Peoples, 1989*

→ See also **Atypical work; Discrimination; Part-time work; Precarious work; Social protection**

Chemicals

The term "chemical" means chemical elements and compounds and mixtures thereof, whether natural or synthetic. Appropriate measures should be taken to prevent or reduce the incidence of chemically induced illnesses and injuries at the workplace. In particular, certain chemicals are harmful to pregnant and nursing mothers and young people.

Detailed regulations exist in many countries concerning the classification systems of chemicals, their labelling and marking, the use of chemical safety data sheets, the responsibilities of suppliers and employers, such as the identification of chemicals, their transfer and disposal, and the exposure of workers. Workers should observe the necessary precautions. Workers are entitled to be informed and trained on the safe use of chemicals, to remove themselves from danger resulting from chemicals at work, to be provided with the necessary physical protection such as masks, boots, gloves, and suits, and to be provided with appropriate medical and biological testing.

Among industrial products, benzene (commonly used as a raw material in industry) is one of the most dangerous. Therefore pregnant women, nursing mothers and young people of both sexes under 18 years of age should not be employed in work processes involving exposure to benzene or products containing benzene.

According to Convention No. 13, the use of white lead, a white pigment used in painting, sulphate of lead, and all products containing these pigments is forbidden in the internal painting of buildings.[5] The employment of young persons under 18 years of age and of all women in painting work of an industrial character involving the use of these products is prohibited. Permitted uses should be regulated by national legislation, and various hygiene measures have to be taken in such cases.

Other instruments have been adopted to protect workers from other specific risks from chemicals such as lead (with specific reference to women and children), white phosphorus and asbestos. The Conclusions on occupational safety and health from the 91st session of the International Labour Conference in 2003 mandated the revision of the standards on benzene, lead poisoning, white phosphorus and white lead.

> *C. 155: Occupational Safety and Health, 1981*
> *R. 171: Occupational Health Services, 1985*
> *C. 162 and R. 172: Asbestos, 1986*
> *C. 167 and R. 175: Safety and Health in Construction, 1988*
> *C. 170 and R. 177: Chemicals, 1990*
> *C. 176: Safety and Health in Mines, 1995*
> *C. 184: Safety and Health in Agriculture, 2001*
> *R. 191: Maternity Protection, 2000*
> *C. 184 and R. 192: Safety and Health in Agriculture, 2001*
> *R. 194: List of Occupational Diseases, 2002*
> *MLC: Maritime Labour Convention, 2006*

→ **See also Health during maternity; Maternity protection; Occupational safety and health; Youth employment**

Childcare and family services and facilities

Childcare and family care are broadly-based concepts covering the provision of public, private, individual or collective services to meet the needs of parents and children or members of the immediate family.

---

[5] This Convention is to be discussed with a view to revision in December 2007.

Making facilities available to enable workers to discharge their responsibilities in all areas of their lives is an important aspect of the promotion of equality of treatment between male and female workers with family responsibilities, and between such workers and other workers. All workers, irrespective of their sex, should have the possibility of combining paid employment with their responsibilities for children and other family members. Sufficient and adequate child-care and family services and facilities, including facilities for breastfeeding mothers, should be provided so that workers with family responsibilities can exercise their right to free choice of employment. These services and facilities should be flexible enough to meet the particular needs of children of different ages and of other family members requiring care. The use of such services and facilities should either be free of charge or set at a reasonable level in accordance with workers' ability to pay.

The improvement of working and living conditions for workers with family responsibilities should be pursued by means of adequate social policies, including measures to be taken by the public authorities. Recommendation No. 165 observes that the competent national authorities should collect and publish adequate statistics on the number of workers with family responsibilities engaged in or seeking employment, and on the number and ages of their children and other dependants requiring care. They should ascertain the needs and preferences so revealed, and on the basis of such information should promote the systematic development of an adequate and appropriate child and family care system. The needs of workers who work unconventional hours and whose children cannot be accommodated in facilities keeping traditional hours should be taken into account.

As employers become more aware of their employees' needs in this respect, many employers, particularly in the developed countries, are voluntarily taking various kinds of action towards the provision of childcare services and facilities for their employees, including on-site or off-site childcare centres, private home day-care agencies, childcare subsidies paid to employees, and information referral services.

C. 156 and R. 165: Workers with Family Responsibilities, 1981

→   See also **Facilities and equipment; Family responsibilities, workers with; Illness in the family, leave for; Parental leave; Work–family balance**

Child labour

Child labour as a form of labour to be eliminated does not signify all forms of employment or work done by children under the age of 18 years. It means work that is detrimental to a child's health, education, welfare or development. The general criteria for defining child labour are the age of the child and the nature of the work. An overriding principle is that work should not interfere with the education and the fullest mental and physical development of the child. Age is a crucial factor because, up to a certain age, the primary occupation of children should be obtaining an education and engaging in other activities appropriate for their healthy development, including play. Children are affected by work differently and more intensely than adults – and the younger the child the greater the vulnerability. The hazardous nature of work and the conditions under which it is carried out are also important criteria.

The ILO estimates that about 218 million children are involved in child labour, 127 million of them engaged in hazardous work, while over 8 million have been forced into work as victims of child trafficking, child soldiers or bonded labourers, or used in illicit activities such as drug trafficking and sexual exploitation (ILO, 2006c, table 1.1).

Child labour is generally associated with poverty and discrimination. It is an issue that not only concerns the human rights of the child but also directly relates to gender discrimination, both because of the unequal role of fathers and mothers as breadwinners and family carers; and because of the different expectations held of girls and boys as regards their education and career prospects. Child labour is also a human resources development problem insofar as it deprives women and men of jobs they might perform more satisfactorily than children and prevents future adult women and men from acquiring skills and exercising rights at work. It thus also prevents the development of equitable employment policies and programmes.

The ILO has been working towards the abolition of child labour since its foundation in 1919. A number of Conventions and Recommendations have been adapted to this end. Convention No. 138 of 1973 stipulates that no child below the age of completing compulsory education (usually 15) may be employed in any economic sector, while Convention No. 182 of 1999 urges immediate action against the worst forms of child labour, such as the use of any girl or boy under 18 in forced labour, armed conflict, prostitution, pornography, or nationally listed hazardous types of work.

National action against child labour must aim at preventing it altogether, as well as withdrawing children from it and providing alternatives. A phased, time-bound, multi-sectoral and integrated strategy including the following steps could be applied:

- creating awareness of the problem nationwide, in communities and work-places;
- carrying out a situation analysis to find out about child labour problems in a country;
- developing and implementing national policies on child labour prevention and elimination;
- strengthening existing organizations and setting up necessary institutional mechanisms;
- motivating a broad alliance of partners to acknowledge and act against child labour;
- promoting the development and application of protective legislation;
- supporting direct action with (potential) child workers;
- removing children from the worst forms of child labour;
- replicating and expanding successful projects;
- mainstreaming child labour issues into national development policies, socio-economic policies such as poverty alleviation and universal education, programmes and budgets.

Child labour affects girls and boys differently. Girls deserve particular attention because discrimination against them frequently results in their being especially vulnerable to exploitation, abuse and the denial of their rights. Girls are more likely:

- to start working at an earlier age;
- to be paid less for the same type of work;
- to be concentrated in sectors and areas characterized by low pay and long hours;
- to be working in sectors which are hidden and unregulated, such as in unpaid family work or domestic service, thus making them more vulnerable to exploitation and abuse;
- to be subject to sexual, physical and emotional abuse;
- to be subject to human trafficking, particularly for purposes of commercial sexual exploitation;
- to be excluded from education altogether or after basic education;

- to be responsible for housework;

- to bear the triple burden of housework, school work and economic work.

Convention No. 182 and Recommendation No. 190 of 1999, on the prohibition and immediate action for the elimination of the worst forms of child labour, specifically stress the need to "take account of the special situation of girls". Some methods for doing so would be:

- to place explicit emphasis on girls as a target group in any action plans or direct action programmes aimed at eliminating child labour;

- to concentrate on those economic sectors where many girls are found (i.e. prostitution, domestic work, agriculture and manufacturing);

- to ensure that, where possible, projects run for "visible working boys" also target "invisible working girls";

- to target the poorest (i.e. single female-headed households) and involve mothers together with fathers in projects for child labourers;

- to link up with efforts to promote education for girls;

- to mobilize women's organizations and activists.

Boys also suffer discrimination in certain situations. They constitute a small majority of the children employed in hazardous work and as child soldiers. In armed conflict, girls tend to be forced to provide sexual services rather than to take part in active combat. Minority cases of boys found in female-dominated occupations, such as domestic work or sexual exploitation, must not be over-looked.

Ideally therefore, gender equality should be mainstreamed into the analysis of child labour and the implementation of measures to eliminate it. This means identifying and assessing the different implications for girls and boys of any planned action and designing actions (policies, legislation, and programmes) in light of such assessment.

> *C. 29: Forced Labour, 1930*
> *C. 138 and R. 146: Minimum Age, 1973*
> *C. 143: Migrant Workers (Supplementary Provisions), 1975*
> *C. 182 and R. 190: Worst Forms of Child Labour, 1999*
> *ILO Declaration on Fundamental Principles and Rights at Work*
> *and its Follow-up, 1998*

➜ See also **Commercial sexual exploitation; Forced labour; Fundamental principles and rights at work; Migrant workers; Trafficking in persons**

Clandestine work

Clandestine work or illegal employment can be defined as a sole or secondary gainful non-casual occupation that is carried out in violation of provisions set by legislation. In particular, it is characterized by non-compliance with labour standards and social security provisions on the part of the employer. Strictly speaking, remunerated work which is not protected through contributions to the social security system should be considered clandestine. However, there are different views of what constitutes clandestine labour in developed and developing countries, reflecting the strength and effectiveness of the relevant legal provisions in each country.

Much clandestine or illegal work is done in the informal economy. However, illegality cannot always be equated with informality (Daza, 2005, p. 2). Informal labour is more likely to be considered clandestine or "hidden" work in the developed countries, whereas in most developing countries, where the majority of people may live in traditional social contexts and may not even be aware of national legislation, informal productive activities are not usually thought of as illegal (Daza, 2005, p. 3).

One of the most worrying aspects of clandestine work is its increasingly strong links to irregular – and often forced – migration. Illegal migration for employment is by no means new, but it is growing at an alarming rate and is increasingly linked with criminal activities such as the traffic in drugs and in human beings, forced prostitution and exploitation in pornography. Many migrants incur large debts with clandestine (and usually criminal) networks in order to slip across borders, and then find themselves forced into clandestine, illegal work in slavery-like conditions in order to repay their debts. Clandestine work is thus often closely related to forced labour.

Although the statistical evidence is not entirely clear, it can be assumed that many clandestine workers are women. For instance, domestic work, rural work and home working, all highly feminized occupations, are particularly hard to regulate and therefore susceptible to clandestine employment. Clandestine work in the sex industry affects women and children in particular. Efforts should be made to ensure, not only that social security contributions are made compulsory for each worker and in all sectors, but that labour inspection and other appropriate national monitoring agencies are enabled to help put an end to abusive working conditions imposed on clandestine workers, particularly migrants, in an irregular labour situation, and to ensure that the workers benefit from recognized rights.

C. 81: Labour Inspection, 1947
C. 97: Migration for Employment (Revised), 1949

R. 86: Migration for Employment (Revised), 1949
C. 143: Migrant Workers (Supplementary Provisions), 1975
C. 150: Labour Administration, 1978
R. 198: Employment Relationship, 2006

➜ See also **Child labour; Forced labour; Home work; Informal economy; Migrant workers; Self-employed workers; Trafficking in persons**

Collective bargaining

Collective bargaining can be an important way to promote gender equality. In most countries it is a principal means of determining terms and conditions of employment, including all aspects of gender equality at work. Equal pay, overtime, hours of work, leave, maternity and family responsibilities, health and the working environment, and dignity at the workplace are all issues for collective bargaining with the potential for promoting gender equality in the workplace. Women's access to career development, promotion and vocational training are also important issues that can be considered in collective bargaining. Not only do gender issues need to be addressed in collective bargaining, but traditional collective bargaining issues, referring to the terms and conditions of employment such as wages, hours of work, working conditions and grievance procedures should be reassessed from a gender perspective. The prerequisite to collective bargaining is freedom of association. Thus, collective bargaining agreements also include the rights and responsibilities of trade unions and employers' organizations.

The subjects for negotiation depend on the social, economic and legal context, and on what women themselves choose as priorities. They might include (inter alia) affirmative action, flexible working hours, pay equity, childcare provision, or sexual harassment. However, gender issues are often not sufficiently dealt with in collective bargaining because women are under-represented in trade union decision-making structures and negotiating teams. Equality clauses are often missing or very limited. The reasons for this may include women's double burden of paid work and domestic labour, which does not leave them enough time to participate in trade union affairs, lack of confidence, assertiveness and training, or the fact that the union is male-dominated and insensitive to women workers' needs (e.g. timing and length of meetings).

For collective bargaining to be truly effective and equitable, the concerns of women must be understood and given credence. Consultation with women workers and ensuring that women are represented on negotiation teams are fundamental ways to do this. Trade unions alone, or the social partners jointly with government, may take initiatives to encourage the inclusion of gender equality issues in social and employment agendas. The ILO can provide information and training to help make collective bargaining more responsive to gender issues.

Men also need certain types of protection with regard to their role in social reproduction. Measures are also necessary to give both men and women the opportunity to share more family responsibilities (e.g. parental leave, flexible working hours and greater access to part-time work).

> *C. 98: Right to Organise and Collective Bargaining, 1949*
> *C. 151: Labour Relations (Public Service), 1978*
> *C. 154 and R. 163: Collective Bargaining, 1981*

→ See also **Family responsibilities, workers with; Freedom of association and the right to organize, Parental leave; Representation and voice; Trade unions; Hours of work**

Commercial sexual exploitation

The ILO's International Programme for the Elimination of Child Labour (ILO/IPEC) uses the term "commercial sexual exploitation" to refer to the use of boys and girls under the age of 18 in prostitution, pornography or other forms of sexual activity in which a child might engage in order to obtain food, shelter or other basic needs. Commercial sexual exploitation of children was defined in the declaration adopted at the First World Congress against Commercial Sexual Exploitation (Stockholm, 1996) as "sexual abuse by the adult and remuneration in cash or kind to the child or a third person or persons. The child is treated as a sexual object and as a commercial object." The commercial sexual exploitation of children is defined as one of the worst forms of child labour by Convention No. 182. Both boys and girls may be victims.

> *C. 29: Forced Labour, 1930*
> *R. 35: Forced Labour (Indirect Compulsion), 1930*
> *C. 105: Abolition of Forced Labour, 1957*
> *C. 182 and R. 190: Worst Forms of Child Labour, 1999*
> *Declaration on Fundamental Principles and Rights at Work, 1998*

→ See also **Child labour; Trafficking in persons**

Computers

With the massive introduction of computers into the workplace, their use is becoming increasingly subject to special rules, collective bargaining, guidelines and decisions on the part of governments, employers' and workers' organizations, and manufacturers. Regulation pertains to both medical risks and the protection of workers' privacy.

Although both men and women work at professional levels in information and communications technology (ICT), repetitive or mechanical work done on-screen, especially in its more recent forms such as remote working, is mainly performed by women. Research indicates that there is some gender differentiation in the effects reported (*Working with VDUs*, 1998).[6]

Most experts agree that workers' health can be affected by excessive work with computers, particularly if the equipment or the environment is poorly designed, the pace of work is tightly controlled, or the opportunities for breaks are restricted. Work with computers can be stressful. There is no agreement, however, as to whether such effects are unique to work with computers or whether they can be attributed to all intensive work.

The most widely recognized effects of working on computers are direct effects on the eyes and musculo-skeletal disorders such as repetitive strain injury (RSI). Some indirect effects appear to be related to stress. Recent World Health Organization (WHO) research has found that non-ionizing radiation is not linked to increased risks for people working at computer screens, and that low-emission computer screens are not linked to increased risk of miscarriage (Paul, 2004, pp. 30, 41). However, several governments, employers and trade unions have adopted a cautious approach to the issue by developing agreements on transfers away from computer work during pregnancy.

The principal measures recommended for protecting the health of computer users are:

- regular breaks or changes in activity when working on-screen (the exact time limits are not specified and a variety of breaks are recommended in practice);

- medical examinations (ophthalmic, neurological and orthopaedic) before the assignment; such examinations should be repeated regularly, at least once a year. If after an examination the operator is declared unsuitable for work with computers, an equivalent job at the same rate of pay should

---

[6] This annotated bibliography lists a number of studies that disaggregate the effects on male and female workers.

be offered and the employer may not dismiss the employee for this reason;

- equipment design that conforms to the appropriate standards and parameters (national or as defined by collective agreements), including the safety of the electrical system and the power supply, as well as appropriate maintenance (i.e. periodic checks of ionizing and non-ionizing radiations emitted by computer screens and printers);

- organization of the working environment (including desks, chairs, room layout, lighting, climate and other physical factors such as noise) according to sound ergonomic criteria;

- training for computer users not only in the use of the equipment itself, but also in the implications of its use on health, safety and ergonomics.

Since many computer users are both women and remote or homeworkers, they do not necessarily benefit from enforcement of the above regulations on computer use.

Work using laptop computers is now very common in office settings as well as among those whose work involves travel and among home-based and self-employed workers. Some of the ergonomic problems regarding desktop computers may be exacerbated in the case of laptops (smaller screens which are harder to see, smaller keyboards causing constricted finger movements, inability to arrange keyboard and screen comfortably, etc.), and the weight of the machine is also a possible hazard.

The mushrooming use of computers and Internet use at work has generated new risks and responsibilities for both employers and workers. While enterprises need to prevent unauthorized access to confidential data (including employees' personal data), a major concern for employees and workers' organizations is the relative ease with which ICT can enable the invasion of workers' privacy through electronic monitoring (e.g. reading email, tracking the duration of telephone calls) and surveillance of workers (e.g. CCTV cameras) both at workplaces and in the context of Remote working. In particular, the possibility that continuous or clandestine monitoring can be used for purposes of bullying or sexual harassment is a cause for concern.

In 1996, the ILO issued a code of practice on the protection of workers' personal data. Although it does not replace national laws and regulations or ILO labour standards, it provides guidance on the protection of such data and makes specific recommendations regarding its collection, storage, and use. While the code does not exclude the monitoring of workers, it restricts it. First, it can be conducted only if the workers concerned are informed in advance. Second, the code emphasizes that clandestine or continuous monitoring should be undertaken only if it is necessary to deal with specific problems related to health and safety or the protection of property (ILO, 1997, para. 6.14, p. 13).

C. 155 and R. 164: Occupational Safety and Health, 1981
R. 194: List of Occupational Diseases, 2002
Protection of Workers' Personal Data: An ILO Code of Practice, 1998

➜   See also **Harassment and pressure; Home work; Occupational health services; Remote working**

Conditions and benefits of employment

All conditions and benefits of employment, including remuneration, invalidity benefit, employment injury benefit, and other benefits, should be made available on equal terms (e.g. pro-rata basis for part-time work) to all employees, irrespective of their sex or other attributes. It should specifically be ensured that:

•   terms, benefits and conditions available to some workers in a particular classification are allocated to all workers in the same or similar classification, irrespective of sex;

•   eligibility for and participation in retirement and pension schemes are allocated on an equal basis;

•   working conditions and work stations are provided on an equitable basis;

•   workers irrespective of sex are protected in the case of invalidity (inability to engage in any gainful activity that is likely to be permanent or that persists after the exhaustion of sickness benefits);

•   workers are insured under an employment injury benefit system in case of an accident or disease resulting from employment.

All employees should be equally informed and kept up to date about the availability of employee benefits and schemes through means such as employee notices, bulletins or announcements.

C. 100 and R. 90: Equal Remuneration, 1951
C. 111 and R. 111: Discrimination (Employment and Occupation), 1958
C. 102: Social Security (Minimum Standards), 1952
C. 128 and R. 131: Invalidity, Old-Age and Survivors' Benefits, 1967
C. 175: Part-Time Work, 1994

➜   See also **Employment injury benefit; Equal remuneration, Equality of opportunity and treatment in employment; Pensions; Survivors' benefit**

Contract compliance

→ See **Affirmative action; Public procurement policies**

Cooperatives

A cooperative is an association of persons who have voluntarily joined together to achieve a common end through forming a democratic organization, making equitable contributions to the capital required and accepting a fair share of the risks and benefits of the undertaking in which the members actively participate. Workers' cooperatives (employee- or worker-owned enterprises) are businesses which are owned and controlled by the members, with membership being open to all employees.

Cooperatives provide an effective organizational means for combining economic and human resources and attaining social benefits. They can be significant vehicles for the empowerment and advancement of women to full equality with men.

A set of Cooperative Principles forms the guidelines whereby the global cooperative movement puts its values into practice. A Statement on Cooperative Identity was adopted at the Centennial Congress of the International Cooperative Alliance (ICA) held in Manchester, United Kingdom, in 1995. The First Cooperative Principle refers to voluntary and open membership and emphasizes that cooperatives are open to all persons who are able to use the services offered by the cooperative and willing to accept the responsibilities of membership without gender discrimination.

Recommendation No. 193 on the Promotion of Cooperatives states: "special consideration should be given to increasing women's participation in the cooperative movement at all levels, particularly at management and leadership levels" (Para. 7 (3)), and that national policies on cooperatives should promote gender equality in cooperatives and their work (Para. 8 (1) (a)). Nonetheless, gender concerns still need to be addressed in cooperatives. Among the main gender-related issues are women's low active participation in cooperatives and their under-representation at decision-making levels. Both are due to a number of economic and socio-cultural factors, gender bias, and legal and political conditions. The traditional role of women in society is probably the largest constraint to their participation in cooperatives and their access to decision-making levels. Women often play a more passive role than men in mixed cooperatives, and men tend to assume leadership roles and are reluctant to share their responsibilities with women.

Cooperative laws and by-laws do not directly discriminate against women since they uphold the principles of open membership and equal rights for members, but they may discriminate indirectly through membership conditions in mixed cooperatives. For example, many agricultural cooperatives accept only owners of land as members, and in some countries women are not legally permitted to own land, even when they cultivate the family property.

A major contribution of women's cooperatives is in the field of savings and credit; but while the majority of members of those cooperatives are women, the administrative posts are traditionally occupied by men.

In many societies, especially where the domains of men and women are separated, women prefer to organize themselves in women-only cooperatives. A major advantage of such cooperatives is that women directly control their economic activities and have the opportunity of gaining leadership and management experience and increased self-confidence. It must, however, be stated that women-only cooperatives have not in general succeeded in changing the subordinate status of women in society and bringing women into mainstream cooperative activities. It is therefore important that viable women's cooperatives are integrated into or affiliated to secondary or apex organizations ensuring that women participate in decision-making and are represented at the management level.

R. 193: Promotion of Cooperatives, 2002

→   See also **Agricultural and other rural workers; Equality of opportunity and treatment in employment; Labour statistics; Representation and voice; Self-employed workers; Women's entrepreneurship**

Cultural identity, respect for

→   See **Diversity in the workplace**

D

Decent work

The elimination of discrimination and the achievement of substantive equality underpin the concept of decent work, whose goal is to achieve productive work for women and men, carried out in conditions of freedom, equity, security and human dignity (Hepple, 2001). Decent work is a fundamental objective of all the ILO's work today. The term "decent work" was first used by the ILO Director-General Juan Somavía as the title of his report for the 87th session of the International Labour Conference in 1999. As the Director-General reiterated on International Women's Day (8 March), 2006, "Decent work is built on respect for fundamental principles and rights at work – including freedom from discrimination." It is necessarily founded upon a framework of rights and responsibilities at work that encourages mutual respect and dialogue and restrains and opposes coercion and discrimination.

The ILO also sees decent work as essential to meeting the Millennium Development Goals and eradicating poverty. Several of the most recent Conventions and Recommendations (since 2002) refer in their preambles to decent work as a primary objective of the ILO.

Gender equality is central to decent work. The ILO estimates that worldwide at least 400 million decent jobs would be needed to satisfy women's demand for decent work (Elder, 2004, p. 3). The Decent Work Agenda is cross-sectoral in nature and is therefore implemented effectively through integrated and coordinated policy and institutional interventions covering the ILO's strategic objectives – the promotion of fundamental rights, employment creation, social protection, and social dialogue. An integrated approach to gender equality and decent work forms a part of this conceptual framework. It means, for example, enhancing equal employment opportunities through measures that also aim to improve women's access to education, skills training and healthcare, while promoting a more equal division of labour in unpaid work and encouraging work–family balance measures related to working time, leave policies, childcare and other family services and facilities for men and women workers with family responsibilities.

→ See also **Gender equality; Millennium Development Goals**

Declaration on Fundamental Principles and Rights at Work

→   See **Fundamental Principles and Rights at Work**

Dependent workers

The concept of the dependent worker arose from the need to give extra protection to workers who depend entirely or mostly on one employer for their source of income but are not in formal full-time employment. It thus falls between the two established concepts of employment and self-employment; but dependent workers are closer to employees than they are to independent contractors because of the link to one main employer although they are not formally employed. They are often similar to employees in a number of ways: they may work on the employer's premises and/or use the employer's equipment and they may perform similar tasks to existing employees or to full-time employees whom they have replaced in an outsourcing arrangement. However, they do not usually benefit from the protections granted to employees on health and safety, hours of work, maternity protection, provisions enabling them to fulfil family responsibilities, or freedom from discrimination.

The 91st session of the ILC (2003), which discussed the employment relationship, recognized that within the framework of the Decent Work Agenda, all workers regardless of their employment status should work in conditions of decency and dignity. This recognition led to the decision to adopt a new standard on the employment relationship in 2006. Recommendation No. 198 addresses this challenge. Recognizing that women workers are among those workers most likely to be affected by uncertain or ambiguous employment relationships and the consequent weak or absent social protection, it enjoins member States to address the gender dimension of such situations in national policy by means of clear policies on gender equality and better enforcement of the relevant laws.

  R. 198: Employment Relationship, 2006

→   See also **Atypical work; Clandestine work; Employment relationship; Home work; Self-employed workers**

Disabilities, workers with

Persons with disabilities are individuals whose prospects of securing, retaining and advancing in suitable employment are substantially reduced as a result of a duly recognized physical or mental impairment. They should have access to suitable employment (including vocational guidance and training) and social integration, in conditions of full participation and equality. They should not be dismissed because of their disability.

Women with disabilities suffer from a double disadvantage, as they often find themselves discriminated against both because they are women and because they are disabled.

Equality of opportunity and treatment for male and female workers with disabilities should be respected and promoted. Special positive measures aimed at ensuring effective equality of opportunity and treatment for workers with disabilities should not be regarded as discriminatory against other workers.

In 2001 the ILO adopted a code of practice on managing disability in the workplace.

> *R. 99: Vocational Rehabilitation (Disabled), 1955*
> *C. 111 and R. 111: Discrimination (Employment and Occupation), 1958*
> *C. 158: Termination of Employment, 1982*
> *C. 159 and R. 168: Vocational Rehabilitation and Employment*
> *(Disabled Persons), 1983*
> *Managing Disability in the Workplace, ILO Code of Practice, 2001*

➜   See also **Affirmative action; Diversity in the workplace**

Disciplinary action

Disciplinary action includes measures taken by the employer against an employee in reaction to non-compliance with her or his obligations. Disciplinary action may include warning, suspension, transfer or demotion.

Policies and procedures should be adopted to ensure that disciplinary action is not taken on an arbitrary or discriminatory basis. The grounds upon which disciplinary action may be taken should be specified, based on objective criteria agreed upon in a social dialogue process, and related to the requirements of the job.

The policies and procedures regarding disciplinary action should be applied equally; no employee should be disciplined for performance or behaviour which is at the same time accepted from other employees.

C. 158 and R. 166: Termination of Employment, 1982
R. 130: Examination of Grievances, 1967
C. 151 and R. 159: Labour Relations (Public Service), 1978

➜ See also **Dismissal**

Discrimination

Discrimination is defined in Convention No. 111 as:

> any distinction, exclusion or preference based on race, colour, sex, religion, political opinion, national extraction or social origin which has the effect of nullifying or impairing equality of opportunity or treatment in employment or occupation (Art. 1 (1a)).

Discrimination is not new and certain forms of discrimination, most notably those on grounds of race or ethnicity and sex, have a long history. More recently, changes in the structure and dynamics of labour markets, themselves responding to broader political, economic and socio-cultural processes, have produced new forms of discrimination based on factors such as HIV-positive status, sexual orientation, employment history or religion. Dealing with discrimination is complicated by the fact that discrimination depends on perceptions and subjective opinions or preconceptions about the abilities or attitudes ascribed to individuals belonging to particular groups, rather than on objective facts, and is often invisible or disguised. Nonetheless, the elimination of discrimination at work is indispensable to any strategy to achieve decent work, reduce poverty and ensure sustainable development. Governments, employers and their organizations, and workers' organizations all have a duty to combat it in the ways appropriate to them.

Discrimination may be *de jure*, meaning that discrimination exists in law, or *de facto*, meaning that it exists in reality or in practice. A labour code providing that women shall receive less pay than men because of their sex would be regarded as de jure discrimination, whereas the actual practice of paying women less would be de facto discrimination.

While cases of direct and de jure sex discrimination have declined over time, de facto discrimination continues to exist or has emerged in new forms. To identify discrimination based on sex, it is therefore advisable to look not only at an intent or purpose reflected in rules or action, but also at the actual effect generated.

An understanding of the distinction between direct and indirect discrimination is useful here. Direct sex discrimination exists when unequal treatment between women and men stems directly from laws, rules or practices making an explicit difference between women and men (e.g. laws which do not allow women to sign contracts but allow men to do so). Indirect sex discrimination happens when rules and practices which appear gender-neutral lead in practice to disadvantages being suffered primarily by persons of one sex. It is often evident not at first glance but only after having analysed the de facto effects of policies or legal provisions, that is, what happens in reality as a result of such rules or practices.

The concept of indirect discrimination shows that the application of the same treatment or requirement to everyone can, in practice, lead to very unequal results. A law, regulation, policy or practice may appear to be "neutral" by not making a distinct difference between women and men, but in fact may result in unequal treatment of persons with certain characteristics. Any treatment that, in practice, leads to disadvantages for the members of just one sex constitutes indirect discrimination if the negative effect is not closely related to the inherent requirements of the job in question. Examples are job requirements or criteria for pay which are seemingly neutral (such as minimum height or weight) but in practice exclude a large percentage of female workers. The intention to discriminate is not a determinant of indirect discrimination. However, employment or hiring practices are not considered to be discriminatory when they are based on the actual and real needs of a job (for instance, political or religious belief may constitute a bona fide qualification for certain positions or occupations; distinctions on the basis of sex may be required for certain jobs, e.g. in the performing arts), or if they are meant to promote equality by affirmative action or to protect women on special grounds such as maternal health. Nevertheless, exclusions of this type must be consistently defined with the requirements of the job and protected by legal review. Distinctions based on individual merit also do not count as discrimination in employment and occupation, but such distinctions are hard to define and open to bias in practice.

Indirect discrimination may also occur when differential treatment is given to particular categories of workers, such as part-time workers. In many countries the exclusion by law of domestic workers, agricultural workers and seasonal workers from social protection is also likely to discriminate against women.

Stereotypical ideas about the distribution of "male" and "female" tasks and capabilities lead to indirect discrimination against women in access to employment and vocational training, especially in technical sectors and career advancement. While the cultural identity of workers should be respected (see p. 46), it must also be recognized that some cultural beliefs and norms about gender roles and relations, for instance about women's right to earn an income or own land, do discriminate against women and contribute to a vicious circle of disadvantage in employment, occupation and pay.

Identifying indirect discrimination enables a critical reassessment of established practices and rules which, though apparently neutral, generate different results for women and men at work. Essential strategies for combating indirect discrimination include:

*   the modification of work organization and distribution of tasks so as to avoid negative effects on the treatment and advancement of women;

*   the adoption of measures (such as social services accessible to all workers) to allow a balance in sharing family and professional responsibilities between the sexes;

*   measures such as sensitization campaigns to combat the use of stereotypes about "male" and "female" tasks and roles.

In most countries, discrimination based on sex is prohibited by law. In practice, however, women in both developing and industrialized countries continue to encounter discrimination in one form or another in their working lives. Other grounds upon which discrimination is prohibited may be included in a country's laws or regulations. In some countries, for example, discrimination in employment is also prohibited on the basis of race or ethnicity, physical or mental disability, age, marital status, maternity, sexual orientation, religion, material well-being or HIV-positive status. In practice, sex discrimination may be compounded by any of these other grounds for discrimination.

The State plays a key role in the elimination of discrimination. Legislation can contribute to this directly by addressing the problem of discrimination at work, and indirectly by guaranteeing equality in matters other than work (such as inheritance, property rights, and education). Laws concerning discrimination at work are being strengthened especially in Europe, while measures to combat indirect sex discrimination are multiplying, as is the establishment of bodies to promote equal opportunities at work. And the process of law-making and reform can be rendered more gender-sensitive by promoting a greater involvement of women as well as men in drafting teams and by adhering to gender-inclusive drafting rules, such as avoiding the outdated concept that masculine forms – such as the pronoun "he" – in a legal text is interpreted to included the feminine "she".

Social dialogue in all its forms (negotiations, consultations and information-sharing) proven its worth in fighting discrimination, as demonstrated by the attention paid to the subject in national pacts, framework and sectoral agreements, and the outcomes of enterprise-level bargaining. The importance of having gender balance in negotiating teams – not only as a way of ensuring that equality issues are not invisible at the bargaining table, but also to infuse the process itself with the skills that both women and men can bring to the bargain – cannot be emphasized strongly enough.

Discrimination, especially in its indirect forms, is slow to change because it reflects prevailing social values which themselves change only slowly. Nonetheless, when sex-discriminatory practices exist in the workplace, women and their representatives should be able to call for the intervention of the public labour inspection service or make a claim with the designated competent authority or court.

> *C. 98: Right to Organise and Collective Bargaining, 1949*
> *C. 111 and R. 111: Discrimination (Employment and Occupation), 1958*
> *C. 117: Social Policy (Basic Aims and Standards), 1962*
> *C. 156 and R. 165: Workers with Family Responsibilities, 1981*
> *C. 169: Indigenous and Tribal Peoples, 1989*
> *ILO Declaration on Fundamental Principles and Rights at Work*
> *and its Follow-up, 1998*

➜ See also **Access to employment; Burden of proof; Employment policy and promotion; Fundamental principles and rights at work; Indigenous and tribal peoples; Labour administration; Labour inspection**

Dismissal

Dismissal is the termination of employment when initiated by the employer. No employment should be terminated without a valid reason (connected with the capacity or conduct of the worker, based on the operational requirements of the undertaking, establishment or service, or resulting from technological and economic structuring) and an appropriate procedure including a guaranteed right of appeal. If there is a serious fault on the part of the worker, if the enterprise closes or the contract of employment expires, the employment can be terminated. However, in such cases, the workers' representative should be consulted.

Workers should not be dismissed for participation in trade union activities or on the basis of race, colour, sex, age (subject to national law and practice regarding retirement), marital status, family responsibilities, pregnancy, religion, political opinion, national extraction, social origin, absence from work during maternity leave, because of short-term illness or injury, or because of compulsory military service or other civic obligations in accordance with national law and practice.

The giving of dismissal notice to a woman when she is away from work on maternity leave or at a time which would mean that the notice would expire

while she is away is not allowed. The period during which the woman is protected from dismissal before and after childbirth should be extended to begin
on the date when the employer is notified of the pregnancy by medical certificate until at least one month after the end of maternity leave.

Where dismissal has been based on discriminatory grounds, reinstatement
should be the primary remedy if desired by the worker. Monetary compensation alone is not a sufficient remedy.

In case of reduction of staff for economic or structural reasons, employees and
their representatives should be consulted and informed of:

*   the number, names and categories of workers likely to be affected;

*   the probable timing of the staff reduction;

*   the selection criteria used in making the decision, before redundancy and
    lay-off decisions are finalized. It should be ensured that the criteria used
    do not disadvantage women to a greater extent than men. This consult-
    ation permits negotiations over the need for and details of the measures
    themselves and can help mitigate the impact of eventual mass dismissals
    using, for example social pacts.

    C. 98: Right to Organise and Collective Bargaining, 1949
    C. 110: Plantations, 1958, and Protocol, 1982
    C. 111 and R. 111: Discrimination (Employment and Occupation), 1958
    C. 154 and R. 163: Collective Bargaining, 1981
    C. 156 and R. 165: Workers with Family Responsibilities, 1981
    C. 158 and R. 166: Termination of Employment, 1982
    C. 171: Night Work, 1990

➡ See also **Burden of proof; Disciplinary action; Marital status;
   Maternity protection; Remedies and sanctions; Sexual harassment**

Diversity in the workplace

Diversity is broadly defined as "the range of values, attitudes, cultural perspec-
tives, beliefs, ethnic background, sexual orientation, skills, knowledge and life
experiences of the individuals making up any given group of people" (European
Commission, 1998, p. 18). However, this general definition crucially assumes
that any group is made up of both males and females and omits gender differences. Diversity in the workplace refers to the differences between workers,
such as sex/gender, race/ethnicity, age, physical and mental ability, socio-economic class, language, religion, nationality, education, sexual orientation,
family/marital status, HIV status, and so on. These differences may be visible

or invisible, and they influence each person's values, beliefs, attitudes, behaviour and life. A diversity approach to the workforce is founded on the premise that harnessing these differences will create a productive environment in which everyone feels that they are valued and their talents and skills are being used optimally, and that this contributes to meeting the organization's goals. A workforce that represents the diversity of a society in terms of gender and other attributes is more likely to understand and respond more effectively to the needs of its customer or client base in that society. Moreover, building and maintaining a diverse workforce with more than token representation of under-represented groups and equitable treatment of all can in itself embody the principles of equality and non-discrimination, helping to defuse prejudices and stereotypes and showing that a society free of discrimination is possible, effective and desirable.

The wide application of the principle of non-discrimination is central to the concept of diversity. Convention No. 111 was originally drawn up to combat a fairly limited range of discriminations enumerated in Article 1.1 (a) (race, colour, sex, religion, political opinion, national extraction or social origin). However, the Convention foresaw in forward-looking Article 1.1 (b) the emergence of other grounds for discrimination that would need to be opposed in the future and left the way open to include in the scope of the Convention:

> such other distinction, exclusion or preference which has the effect of nullifying or impairing equality of opportunity or treatment in employment or occupation as may be determined by the Member concerned after consultation with representative employers' and workers' organisations, where such exist, and with other appropriate bodies.

Accordingly, many new grounds have been incorporated in various national legislations since the Convention was adopted, including age, sexual orientation, place of birth, legitimacy of parentage, physical or mental health, medical history, real or perceived HIV status, family relationship with other workers in the enterprise, educational level, language, accent, physical appearance, criminal record, status with regard to public assistance, and atypical hereditary cellular or blood trait.

Equality between women and men is clearly a key component of diversity. However, care needs to be taken that gender is not absorbed into diversity and that its intersection with other aspects of diversity is analysed and taken into account in policy formulation and implementation so that gender equality and women's rights do not disappear. Intersectionality is an analytical concept that illuminates the ways in which gender interacts with other identities (race/ethnicity, socio-economic class, ability, age, sexual orientation, religion, HIV-positive status, etc.) and hence shows how gender inequality and discrimination interact with other inequalities and discriminations to structure a person's relative position of privilege or disadvantage in society. Intersectionality is a useful approach when working to understand and address multiple (and often indirect) discrimination and to create and manage a diverse workforce with equity.

A diversity approach also requires recognition of, and due respect for, all workers' cultural identity, religious practices, linguistic abilities, national origin, political opinion or other characteristics. All cultural, religious, linguistic and other related needs of the workforce should be identified and policies should be adopted with regards to the need to prevent discrimination in employment, so as to permit:

• observance of religious holidays and prayer or meditation times;

• observance of a culture-specific mourning period for a deceased relative;

• observance of special dietary regimes and medical practices;

• wearing of traditional and faith-based dress, beards and hairstyles;

• the provision, where appropriate, of language training, interpretation and translation facilities in all areas of personnel management and human resource development.

However, care needs to be taken to ensure that attention to cultural needs and values does contradict universal principles of respect for the rights of women.

> *C. 111 and R. 111: Discrimination (Employment and Occupation), 1958*
> *C. 143: Migrant Workers (Supplementary Provisions), 1975*
> *C. 169: Indigenous and Tribal Peoples, 1989*
> *R. 104: Indigenous and Tribal Populations, 1957*
> *R. 195: Human Resources Development, 2004*

➜ See also **Access to employment; Discrimination; Indigenous and tribal peoples; Migrant workers; Selection procedures**

Division of labour

From an economist's viewpoint, the division of labour is the process whereby workers are allocated to the activity in which they are deemed to be the most productive. It may be based on:

• technical characteristics, when a single production process is broken down into its constituent parts, each part being performed by a different person or machine; or

- social characteristics, when people are allocated to specific tasks on the basis of their physical or social characteristics, such as age, sex, race, religion, ethnic origin or social class.

The division of labour by gender refers primarily to the segregation of paid and unpaid work between women and men in private and public life. This division reflects the traditional division between women's and men's roles in society, whereby women assumed the bulk of family care and domestic functions, while men were ascribed the primary responsibility for the family's economic or financial well-being as (usually sole) breadwinners in continuous, full-time, lifelong employment. However, it is now accepted that this distinction does not reflect the current reality of men's and women's lives and that it results in women's work often being invisible and therefore undervalued in national accounts and under-represented in the labour market.

Combating sex discrimination and the active promotion of gender equality means changing attitudes, practices and policies that reinforce the traditional gender division of labour. Recommendation No. 165 (Para. 11(b)) enjoins competent national authorities to promote education to encourage more equal sharing of family responsibilities. Changing the traditional role of men as well as that of women is a concern expressed in the Preamble to Convention No. 156, recalling the Preamble to the UN Convention on the Elimination of All Forms of Discrimination against Women (CEDAW, 1979). Research in the field of masculinities focuses on the changing roles of men and boys and particularly on the desirability of adapting work schedules and career patterns to enable men to develop closer relationships with their children. This field of research emphasizes that equality between the sexes also demands urgent attention to measures which challenge and change contemporary expectations of men and boys.

C. 156 and R. 165: Workers with Family Responsibilities, 1981

→ See also **Family responsibilities, workers with; Female-headed households; Gender; Gender analysis; Masculinities; Occupational segregation; Work–family balance**

Domestic workers

Domestic work is the housework and gardening undertaken by employees who may or may not be family members to facilitate the running of domestic life and the meeting of personal needs. The vast majority of domestic workers are female, and increasingly they are migrant women. Many are girl children; in Tanzania, for instance, the recruitment of girls under 14 years of age from rural areas to work as domestics in the cities has been a concern for ILO/IPEC (ILO, SEAPAT, 1998).

Workers assigned to the cleaning of public and private buildings are not classified as domestic workers. Au pairs and nannies employed through agencies are covered by Convention No. 181 and Recommendation No. 188 on private employment agencies.

Domestic work can be done full-time (on either a residential or a non-residential basis), part-time or on a casual basis by the hour. Though the tasks performed are in many cases the same as those performed in housework carried out by family members, the relationship is that of employment, and all but a few countries have some kind of regulatory framework for domestic work. Many have special labour regulations and social security schemes for domestic workers. In principle, pay and social benefits such as pension contributions, maternity and sick leave, weekly rest and paid holidays have to be granted in accordance with national law. The remuneration must be proportional to the quantity and type of work, and can be paid monthly, weekly or daily; pay for migrant workers must be the same as for local workers. In practice, special labour regulations involve many exceptions which are less favourable to domestic workers. The invisibility of domestic work makes it difficult to regulate, although many labour administrations extend their outreach into this area of the world of work.

Domestic workers generally face multiple problems: long hours of work; heavy workload; low salaries; exclusion from health schemes and cash benefits or protection against dismissal in case of maternity; lack of control by the authorities responsible for labour inspection and law enforcement; a weak collective bargaining position; and a high level of control by the employer. Resident domestic workers face additional problems of isolation, difficulty in organizing, a regimented lifestyle, poor living quarters, insufficient food, and lack of privacy. Violence at work, either physical or psychological, is also a common work hazard with which domestic workers are confronted.

A few ILO Conventions contain clauses that explicitly include or exclude domestic workers from their scope, but no Convention deals specifically with domestic workers. In general, ILO standards that are applicable to other categories of workers also apply to domestic workers. This is valid in particular for their rights to equal opportunity and treatment, to organization and collective bargaining, to health insurance, and to observance of the minimum working age. Other Conventions contain flexibility clauses allowing the ratifying countries to exclude particular categories of workers or establishments; this applies, for instance, to domestic workers' unemployment provision and restrictions concerning night work done by young people.

Domestic work is distinct from home work and is not covered by the Home Work Convention, 1996 (No. 177).

> *C. 95 and R. 85: Protection of Wages, 1949*
> *C. 100 and R. 90: Equal Remuneration, 1951*

C. 103: Maternity Protection (Revised) and R. 95: Maternity Protection, 1952
C. 175: Part-Time Work, 1994
C. 181 and R. 188: Private Employment Agencies
C. 183 and R. 191: Maternity Protection, 2000
R. 198: Employment Relationship, 2006

➡ See also **Fundamental principles and rights at work; Maternity protection; Migrant workers; Social protection; Social security; Violence at work, gender-based; Hours of work**

E

Early retirement

→   See **Older women workers; Pensions**

Economic activity

Statisticians use the term "economic activity" rather than "work". The definition of economic activity has broadened over the years to cover the supply of labour for the production of economic goods and services as defined by the United Nations System of National Accounts (SNA). The economically active population includes persons who actually produce goods and services, as well as those who are willing and available to do so, but do not produce them. The SNA includes the production of goods and services for the market and the production of goods in households for their own consumption, but excludes unpaid services for the consumption of the household that produces them. These services are commonly known as "housework", including activities such as cooking, cleaning, and caring for children and other family members.

The ILO defines economic activity as "all work for pay or in anticipation of profit" and specifies that the production of economic goods and services includes the production and processing of agricultural products and the production of other goods for home consumption.

Although the proportion of women who are economically active has been rising over the last decades, women's participation in economic activities has been, and still is, substantially underestimated in all regions of the world, even if the economic contribution of unpaid housework is not included.

→   See also **Housework; Labour force; Labour market; Labour statistics**

Economically active population

→   See **Labour force**

Education

Women and girls in most parts of the world continue to face obstacles to their effective participation in education and training as a result of their gender-determined roles (housework, caring for family members, and early marriage and child-bearing). This form of discrimination calls for deliberate policy measures aimed at ensuring equal access to, and equal opportunities in, the acquisition and maintenance of education and skills by both males and females. Not only should education, vocational guidance and training, and lifelong learning[7] be open to men and women equally from primary education onwards, but boys and girls ought to be brought up to understand the pressures of gender-specific prejudices and to aspire to occupations and careers which are not gender-stereotyped. This kind of education is no less important for boys than for girls.

Considerable progress has been made in nearly all countries in increasing access to education especially for girls. Gender gaps in educational attainment are narrowing, not least as a result of efforts to meet the third Millennium Development Goal, which refers specifically to making progress towards gender equality and the empowerment of women by means of eliminating gender disparity in education. However, there is evidence that higher educational attainment does not automatically translate into reductions in labour market inequalities. Equality of opportunity between young men and women, once they have left formal education, must be ensured in vocational guidance and training and access to employment.

ILO/IPEC views education, and in particular girls' education, as a key strategy towards the elimination and prevention of child labour.

> C. 111 and R. 111: Discrimination (Employment and Occupation), 1958
> C. 122: Employment Policy, 1964
> R. 169: Employment Policy (Supplementary Provisions), 1984
> C. 88: Employment Service, 1948
> C. 142: Human Resources Development, 1975
> R. 195: Human Resources Development, 2004

➜ See also **Child labour; Division of labour; Equal remuneration; Glass ceiling; Millennium Development Goals; Non-traditional occupations; Occupational segregation; Vocational training; Youth employment**

---

[7] Defined in Human Resources Development Recommendation, 2004 (No. 195), as encompassing all learning activities undertaken throughout life for the development of competencies and qualifications.

Elder care

As life expectancy rises and the world's population ages, more and more workers in all regions are caring for elderly or disabled parents or relatives. Governments have come to realize that the growing number of elderly people requiring care represents a potentially huge financial burden on the State. The management of elder care and its division between the public and private spheres is the subject of an evolving debate.

Elder care is implicitly covered in Convention No. 156 and Recommendation No. 165, and some states are introducing measures for elder care consistent with the provisions of the Convention. In some industrialized countries, for instance the United States, Canada and Australia, a variety of programmes have been established to assist working family members who are caring for elderly relatives. In other countries programmes are geared more to the elderly themselves than to workers' needs for assistance with elder care, but the existence of such programmes can perhaps be considered a starting point for programmes directed more towards the needs of working carers. In a few countries employers contribute to the financing of facilities that meet workers' needs for such care (ILO, 1993b, Ch. 5).

The same issues concerning gender equality apply to elder care as to other family responsibilities. Women and men should be given equal opportunity to respond to the needs of elderly relatives, and where women continue to be the principal carers in practice, this should not count against them in access to employment, pay or career advancement.

C. 156 and R. 165: Workers with Family Responsibilities, 1981

→   See **Care work; Childcare and family services and facilities; Family responsibilities, workers with; Illness in the family, leave for**

Employability

The term "employability" relates to the portable skills, competencies and qualifications that enhance an individual's capacity to make use of available education and training opportunities in order to secure and retain decent work, to progress in an enterprise and between jobs, and to cope with changing conditions in technology and the labour market. These skills and competencies also need to be upgraded or updated throughout the working life.

Through its Skills and Employability Department, the ILO promotes the improvement of and investment in training policies and programmes worldwide, with special emphasis on training strategies that support the integration of groups that may be disadvantaged in the labour market. These groups include women, people with disabilities, older workers and young workers.

Relevant policy areas in which gender-sensitive approaches are beneficial include:

- Investment in education and training, particularly in developing countries, and particularly for women and groups with special needs, such as people with disabilities;

- Basic education, literacy and core skills, particularly in the poorest countries, and with an emphasis on girls' education and skills training;

- Vocational education and training systems, with an emphasis on avoiding sex-stereotyped or occupationally segregated provision of vocational training;

- Recognizing skills acquired from a wide range of sources some of which may be non-traditional. The lifelong learning approach means that all kinds of learning – formal, non-formal and informal – should be recognized and made visible. This is important for women whose skills are more likely to have been developed outside formal training institutions;

- Promoting social dialogue on gender equity in training, human resources development and lifelong learning;

- Active labour market programmes, including effective approaches to skills acquisition and development in formal and informal settings for people who are disadvantaged in the labour market, including women and girls.

- Reforming employment services and promoting cooperative efforts between public and private employment agencies towards the promotion of equality of opportunity and treatment in access to employment and to particular occupations, and a concerted approach to the avoidance of discrimination.

C. 181 and R. 188: Private Employment Agencies, 1997
R. 195: Human Resources Development, 2004

→ See also **Access to employment; Education; Vocational guidance; Vocational training**

Employee

An employee is a worker in the public or private sector who receives remuneration resulting from a contract of employment in return for work done or services rendered to an employer or a person designated by the employer. An employee is distinguished from a self-employed or own-account worker or an independent contractor by factors which might include the following:[8]

- the work is carried out according to the instructions and under the control of another party;

- the work involves the integration of the worker in the organization of the enterprise;

- the work is performed solely or mainly for the benefit of another person and must be carried out personally by the worker;

- the work is carried out within specific working hours or at a workplace specified or agreed by the party requesting the work;

- remuneration is paid periodically to the worker and constitutes the worker's sole or principal source of income;

- entitlements such as weekly rest and annual holidays are recognized;

- the work does not involve any financial risk for the worker.

This kind of employment relationship is regulated not only by international and national labour standards but also, in many countries, by collective agreements. Besides her or his economic rights (remuneration, social security contribution, allowances), the employee should have a series of rights concerning her or his freedom and dignity:

- trade union rights;

- civil and political rights;

- just and decent conditions of work;

- freedom from discrimination on grounds of sex or other personal attributes;

- respect for private life and consideration of the need for work–family balance.

An employer has no right to inquire into employees' private lives, political opinions, religion, or participation in union activities (see *Employer*, p. 65 and *Tripartism*, p. 184).

---

[8] See Employment Relationship Recommendation, 2006 (No. 198), Art. 13.

C. 87: *Freedom of Association and Protection of the Right to Organise, 1948*
C. 98: *Right to Organise and Collective Bargaining, 1949*
C. 122 *and R.* 122: *Employment Policy, 1964*
C. 141 *and R.* 149: *Rural Workers' Organisations, 1975*
C. 151: *Labour Relations (Public Service), 1978*
C. 154: *Collective Bargaining, 1981*
R. 159: *Labour Relations (Public Service), 1978*
R. 198: *Employment Relationship, 2006*

➜   See also **Collective bargaining; Employer; Employment relationship; Freedom of association and the right to organize; Trade unions**

Employer

An employer is any person or organization for whom a person performs work or renders any service and receives payment as an employee.

Individual employers or enterprises, as well as employers' and workers' organizations and governments, have a responsibility to combat discrimination in the workplace. Both employers' and workers' organizations have a responsibility to identify and recognize existing discriminatory practices and to combat these through all their activities, starting within their own organizations. Employers have no right to inquire into employees' private lives, political opinions, religion, or participation in union activities.

In particular, employers have a responsibility to promote gender equality in their enterprises and in employers' organizations, including equal pay for work of equal value. The promotion of equality is, in fact, not only a question of respecting rights and the law, but it is also good business practice. An enterprise that is seen not to be taking equality seriously (for instance, by not having an equal opportunities policy or not acting on an existing policy) may risk losing high-quality employees and may be less attractive to potential clients. In the case of public procurement, failure to demonstrate attention to equality can result in lost contracts.

Women make up a minority (albeit a gradually growing one) of employers and managers for many reasons. In society at large, they may have to contend with fewer opportunities for education and training; occupational segregation in education, training and employment; lower access to credit; and persistent stereotyped attitudes against women in management roles. In the workplace itself, obstacles include;

•   biased recruitment and promotion systems and procedures;

•   mobility requirements (women are less likely than men to be able to relocate or travel for work at short notice);

- seniority requirements (women often lose seniority through career discontinuities due to maternity);

- the influence of male networks ("old boys' clubs") on promotion;

- long hours of work expected of senior staff;

- job design involving lower skill requirements for "women's jobs", combined with lower access to in-service training / lifelong learning;

- incompatibility between the expectations of management and family responsibilities;

- weak enforcement of equality policies.

    C. 87: Freedom of Association and Protection of the Right to Organise, 1948
    C. 98: Right to Organise and Collective Bargaining, 1949
    C. 100 and R. 90: Equal Remuneration, 1951
    C. 111 and R. 111: Discrimination (Employment and Occupation), 1958
    C. 122 and R. 122: Employment Policy, 1964
    C. 151 and R. 159: Labour Relations (Public Service), 1978
    R. 198, Employment Relationship, 2006

→ See also **Employee; Employers' organizations; Employment relationship; Glass ceiling; Public procurement**

Employers' organizations

Employers have the right to establish and to join organizations of their own choice with a view to furthering and defending their collective interests. Public authorities should refrain from any interference which would restrict this right. The range and content of employers' collective interests vary widely, so the structure, membership basis and functions of employers' organizations differ widely between countries. Employers' organizations are one of the constituents of the ILO which engages in social dialogue, including bipartite and tripartite negotiations and consultation.

In order to overcome the continuing cultural, social and economic obstacles to women's opportunities to become employers or managers, employers' organizations ought to focus on:

- encouraging equality in employment, including equal pay for work of equal value;

- increasing the participation of women managers and business entrepreneurs;

- expanding education for work and vocational training, particularly for the educationally disadvantaged;

- increasing opportunities for competitive and productive positions.

There is a broad range of means of action, initiatives and activities that employers' organizations can undertake to promote gender equality. They can raise awareness among their members, both lower-level federations and individual employers, of the importance of adopting a more proactive approach to gender equality and the benefits of such an approach. The business case for greater equality is by now well established. Equal opportunities employers argue that greater equality at work is in their business interest for a number of reasons:

- They benefit from the widest possible pool of talent from which to select their employees;

- Non-discriminatory employment may attract better candidates;

- The selection process of employees is more credible when it is transparent and based on merit;

- If its staffing is diverse, the business is likely to benefit from a diversity of experiences and skills;

- Being known as an equal opportunities employer can promote a good public image;

- The process of developing and adopting a company equal opportunities policy offers a useful chance to review existing policies and practices, strengthen employee communication and consultation procedures, and build up confidence and company loyalty (ILO, Bureau for Employers' Activities, 2005, pp. 9–10).

Employers' organizations can promote gender equality in the workplace by:

- engaging in discussions of legislative and other equality measures;

- becoming members of national bodies responsible for gender issues;

- developing voluntary codes of practice and other forms of voluntary commitment;

- conducting surveys and studies and disseminating information on gender issues;

- offering policy advice to members and preparing guidance materials;

- training, networking and mentoring;

- setting up women's committees or other bodies within employers' organizations.

C. 87: Freedom of Association and Protection of the Right to Organise, 1948
C. 98: Right to Organise and Collective Bargaining, 1949
C. 100 and R. 90: Equal Remuneration, 1951
C. 122 and R. 122: Employment Policy, 1964
C. 154: and R. 163: Collective Bargaining, 1981
R. 189: Job Creation in Small and Medium-Sized Enterprises, 1998

➜ See also **Collective bargaining; Diversity; Freedom of association and the right to organize; Social dialogue; Tripartism; Tripartite consultation**

Employment injury benefit

All workers, irrespective of sex or other personal attributes, should be insured in case of an accident or disease resulting from employment. Convention No. 121 (Art. 1) specifies that:

National legislation concerning employment injury benefits shall protect all employees, including apprentices, in the public and private sectors, including co-operatives, and, in respect of the death of the breadwinner, prescribed categories of beneficiaries.

The contingencies covered by the employment injury benefit system are:

• medical care to maintain, restore or improve the ability to work;

• incapacity for work involving suspension of earnings;

• total or partial permanent loss of earning capacity;

• loss of support suffered by dependants resulting from death.

In the case of incapacity for work, total loss of earning capacity or the death of a breadwinner, the benefit should be a periodical payment.

These benefits should apply equally to women and men, but in practice this is often not the case. National policies and institutional mechanisms should aim at creating effective equality of treatment between men and women workers in this respect. Some governments (e.g. India) have put structures in place to ensure that various social security benefits, including employment injury benefit, are available to unorganized workers, including women workers.

C. 102: Social Security (Minimum Standards), 1952
C. 121 and R. 121: Employment Injury Benefits, 1964
R. 194: List of Occupational Diseases, 2002

➜ See also **Conditions and benefits of employment; Social protection; Social security**

Employment-intensive works programmes

Employment-intensive works programmes (EIPs) are infrastructure development programmes (public works programmes to meet basic needs in rural, urban and suburban areas) financed by public investment with the objective of creating and maintaining employment and incomes. EIPs may serve both to reduce poverty and to meet basic needs in areas of widespread unemployment and underemployment. Special attention should be paid to creating employment opportunities for women, youth and other disadvantaged groups.

Workers for EIPs are to be recruited on a voluntary basis and not diverted from other productive activities. The conditions of employment offered should be consistent with national law and practice. Legal provisions governing access to employment, hours of work, remuneration, holidays with pay, occupational safety and health, and social security should be guaranteed, and programmes of vocational training should be provided.

Special efforts should be made through promotional, information and capacity-building programmes to provide equal access for poor women, and to ensure equal remuneration for work of equal value. The abuse of women's "voluntary" unpaid labour as part of the communities' contribution should be combated. Appropriate childcare and transport facilities (when long distances are involved) constitute positive incentives for enhancing poor women's participation in EIPs.

R. 169: Employment Policy (Supplementary Provisions), 1984

➜ See also **Employment injury benefit; Family benefit; Conditions and benefits of employment; Maternity protection; Pension; Old-age benefit; Survivors' benefit**

Employment policy and promotion

The basic aim of employment policy is to achieve and maintain a high level of productive and freely chosen employment.[9] Employment promotion is aimed at increasing the number of employed people and reducing the number of unemployed. Convention No. 122 provides a framework to guide employment policy interventions that seek to reduce poverty and promote development without discrimination.

---

[9] The concept of productive employment is based on the idea that no society can afford to waste the capabilities of any of its members.

There should be work for all who are available for and seeking it, such work should be as productive as possible, and there should be freedom of choice of employment. All workers irrespective of their sex should have the fullest possible opportunity to qualify for jobs for which they are suited and use their skills in them. Discrimination, including discrimination on grounds of sex, is not permitted.

An active employment policy should be designed and carried out so as to promote decent work – full, productive and freely chosen employment. Such a policy should help to stimulate economic growth and development, raise levels of living, meet personnel requirements and overcome unemployment and underemployment. Population and welfare programmes aimed at improving the economic status of particularly vulnerable groups such as migrant women, female-headed households and young pregnant women may further enhance the situation of many women workers.

Employment policy should take due account of the stage and level of economic development of a country or region. Representatives of the persons who are affected by the measures to be taken, and in particular representatives of employers and workers, should be consulted.

> *C. 122 and R. 122: Employment Policy, 1964*
> *R. 169: Employment Policy (Supplementary Provisions), 1984*

➡ See also **Labour administration; Public employment services and private employment agencies**

Employment relationship

The employment relationship is the legal link between employers and employees. It exists when a person performs work or services under certain conditions in return for remuneration (ILO 2006b, p. 3). [10]

It is through the employment relationship, however it is defined, that reciprocal rights and obligations are created between employee and employer. It has been and continues to be the main vehicle through which workers gain access to the rights and benefits associated with employment in the areas of labour law and social security. The existence of an employment relationship is the condition that determines the application of the labour and social security law provisions addressed to employees. It is the key point of reference for determining the nature and extent of employers' rights and obligations towards their workers.

---

[10] This report deals in depth with the employment relationship in law and practice, covering about 60 member States spanning different regions, legal systems and traditions.

It is particularly important that the employment relationship be accountable, transparent, fair and equitable in view of the increasing number of dependent workers who lack protection because of one or more of the following factors, often in combination:

- the scope of the law is too narrow, or it is too narrowly interpreted;

- the law is poorly or ambiguously formulated so that its scope is unclear;

- the employment relationship is disguised;

- the relationship is objectively ambiguous, giving rise to doubt as to whether or not an employment relationship really exists;

- the employment relationship clearly exists but it is not clear who the employer is, what rights the worker has and who is responsible for them;

- there is a lack of compliance and enforcement.

Accordingly, questions such as the following need to be asked:

- When does an employment relationship exist?

- What is an ambiguous employment relationship?

- What is a disguised employment relationship?

- What is a multi-party or "triangular" employment relationship?

- Who is an employee?

- Who is an employer?

Recommendation No. 198 on the employment relationship contains several references to gender equality and non-discrimination. In Article 5, it stipulates that "Members should take particular account in national policy to ensure effective protection to workers especially affected by the uncertainty as to the existence of an employment relationship, including women workers, as well as the most vulnerable workers, young workers, older workers, workers in the informal economy, migrant workers and workers with disabilities". Article 6 enjoins member States to "take special account in national policy to address the gender dimension in that women workers predominate in certain occupations and sectors where there is a high proportion of disguised employment relationships, or where there is a lack of clarity of an employment relationship" and to have "clear policies on gender equality and better enforcement of the relevant laws and agreements at national level so that the gender dimension can be effectively addressed".

R. 198: Employment Relationship, 2006

→ See also **Atypical work; Dependent workers; Employee; Employer; Flexibility of labour; Home work; Informal economy; Migrant workers; Older women workers; Part-time workers; Precarious work; Remote working; Self-employed workers; Trafficking in persons**

Equality of opportunity and treatment in employment and occupation

Equality of opportunity and equality of treatment are two complementary aspects of equality in employment and occupation. Equal opportunity means having an equal chance to apply for a particular job to be employed, to attend educational or training courses, to be eligible to attain certain qualifications and to be considered as a worker or for a promotion in all occupations or positions, including those dominated by one sex or the other. Equal treatment refers to equal entitlements in pay, working conditions, security of employment, reconciliation between work and family life, and social protection. The reference to both employment and occupation means that protection from discrimination is provided not only to employees but also to other segments of the labour force, such as own-account or self-employed workers, owners of enterprises and unpaid family workers.

The promotion of equality in employment is a step beyond the prohibition or elimination of discrimination (which can be described as "negative" equality, consisting merely of the absence of inequality) to a more proactive, positive approach. It requires continuous efforts, including the implementation of concrete, adequately resourced measures and regular monitoring and evaluation.

Equality of opportunity and treatment in occupation refers in particular to the breaking down of horizontal and vertical occupational segregation.

> *C. 100 and R. 90: Equal Remuneration, 1951*
> *C. 111 and R. 111: Discrimination (Employment and Occupation), 1958*
> *C. 156 and R. 165: Workers with Family Responsibilities, 1981*

→ See also **Access to employment; Affirmative action, Burden of proof; Conditions and benefits of employment; Discrimination; Employee; Equal remuneration; Family responsibilities, workers with; Fundamental principles and rights at work; Occupational segregation; Remedies and sanctions; Social protection**

Equal remuneration

Remuneration is defined in Convention No. 100 (Art. 1 (a)) as "the ordinary, basic or minimum wage or salary and any additional emoluments whatsoever, payable directly or indirectly, whether in cash or in kind, by the employer to the worker and arising out of the worker's employment".

The principle of equal pay for work of equal value addresses discriminatory structural gender biases in labour markets which lead to horizontal and vertical occupational segregation by sex (see p. 144). It means that rates and types of remuneration should be based not on an employee's sex (or other personal attributes) but on an objective evaluation of the work performed. This is a fundamental women workers' right, widely acknowledged and implemented in national legal systems. Nonetheless, statistics and research indicate a persistent pay differential between the sexes which has decreased only slightly in recent years. On average worldwide, women's income per hour worked is about 75 per cent of men's.

Several reasons for these differences in earnings are usually cited. Differences in skills and qualifications, seniority, and sectors of employment all have an influence, although, contrary to conventional belief, women's lower educational attainments and interrupted career paths are not the main reason for gender differentials in pay. Discrimination is a more important determinant. Because pay structures and job classification systems are biased, the jobs done by most women tend to be classified at lower levels. Women are highly concentrated in "flexible" work such as part-time, piece-rate or temporary work, which are usually poorly paid. Women work fewer overtime hours than men. At the same time, the costs of employing a woman are perceived to be higher than those of employing a man.

Discrimination operates in access to promotion which affects pay, and fringe benefits. Detecting discrimination in remuneration is not easy, since the factors accounting for a gender gap in pay have to be identified in order to determine whether or not they constitute discrimination. In many countries there is a shortage of reliable statistics for measuring pay gaps. However, where women's pay is typically lower than men's in a particular occupation, sector, skill level or pension level, it is worth looking for possible discrimination in pay.

Recognition of the right to equal pay for work of equal value is recognized in the ILO's Constitution (1919). Convention No. 100, adopted in 1951, is a specific instrument concerning equal remuneration for work of equal value, covering the basic wage and any additional cash or in-kind remuneration or benefit arising out of the worker's employment. The Resolution on Gender Equality, Pay Equity and Maternity Protection, adopted by the 92nd Session of the ILC in 2004, seeks to strengthen the Convention and promote its wider ratification and application, and also calls on the social partners to carry out capacity-building, training and advocacy programmes on all aspects of pay equity.

However, both employers and trade unions tend to give pay equity a lower priority than other issues such as pay levels, job creation and employment. Trade unions also often tend to see pay equity as an issue for women workers only, not as a strategic issue for all workers.

Application of the principle of equal pay for work of equal value is the joint responsibility of the State and the social partners. It may be applied by means of:

- national laws or regulations;

- legally established or recognized machinery for wage determination;

- collective agreements between employees and workers;

- or a combination of these (Convention No. 100, Art. 2).

Practical measures for its implementation include the following:

- Job classification systems and pay structures should be based on objective criteria, irrespective of the sex of the people who do the job.

- Any reference to a particular sex should be eliminated in all remuneration criteria, in collective agreements, pay and bonus systems, salary schedules, benefit schemes, medical coverage and other fringe benefits.

- Any remuneration system or structure which has the effect of grouping members of a particular sex in a specific job classification and salary level should be reviewed and adjusted to ensure that other workers are not performing work of equal value in a different job classification and salary level.

Programmes and other measures should be adopted in the workplace to implement the principle of equal remuneration. It should be ensured that:

- corrective measures are developed and applied whenever a situation of unequal remuneration is discovered;

- special training programmes are organized to inform staff, particularly supervisors and managers, of the need to pay employees on the basis of the value of the work and not of who is performing the work;

- separate negotiations on equal remuneration are conducted between management, employees' representatives and the women workers affected by the existing unequal job classification or pay structure of a particular workplace.

Part-time and hourly employees should be remunerated on an equal basis with full-time employees proportional to the number of hours they work.

> *C. 100 and R. 90: Equal Remuneration, 1951*
> *C. 175 and R. 182: Part-Time Work, 1994*
> *ILO Resolution on Gender Equality, Pay Equity and Maternity Protection, 2004*

➜   See also **Collective bargaining; Conditions and benefits of employment; Discrimination; Fundamental principles and rights at work; Job evaluation and classification; Occupational segregation**

Equity

➜   See **Gender equity**

Export processing zones

Export processing zones (EPZs) are areas designated for receiving, storing and processing or assembling goods without the obligation to pay duties. They typically offer special incentives to attract foreign investment, and the materials imported into them undergo a certain degree of processing before being re-exported. EPZs are now a very common feature of the globalized economy, employing as many as 50 million workers worldwide in 2004 (ILO and World Commission on the Social Dimension of Globalization, 2004, p. 111). For countries where they operate, they are a vital entry point into the global manufacturing economy, providing a valuable source of investment, employment and technological know-how. However, while EPZs are a major and growing source of jobs, labour relations and human resource development remain neglected areas. Their tenuous linkages with the domestic economies of the host countries and the fact that they are often exempted from compliance with national labour or environmental legislation make it easy for them to disregard workers' rights.

The workforce in EPZs is composed mainly of women (up to 90 per cent) in the younger age groups. They work in a number of product sectors, but occupational segregation is high; for example in the textile and garment industries, there is a demand for female in preference to male labour in the (relatively low-value) textile and garment industries. EPZs provide a significant opportunity for young women workers to enter the formal economy, but many get locked into low-skilled and low-wage jobs because of direct or indirect discrimination.[11]

---

[11] For more information on the impact of EPZs on women's employment, see ILO. 2003. *Employment and social policy in respect of export processing zones (EPZs)*, Governing Body, 286th Session, Geneva, Mar., GB.286/ESP/3.

The enterprises involved should therefore make special efforts to ensure that women workers are not discriminated against in terms of salary or access to training and promotion. Women workers should enjoy maternity protection and be provided with maternity leave, employment security during pregnancy and maternity leave, and nursing breaks and facilities. Measures should be taken to help them combine work and family responsibilities (limitation of excessive hours of work and night work, childcare facilities, etc.). Discriminatory hiring policies such as pregnancy tests for job applicants should be outlawed. Policies and procedures should be in place to prevent and deal with sexual harassment. Free, strong and representative workers' organizations have a major role to play in order to improve the working conditions in these zones.

C. 87: Freedom of Association and Protection of the Right to Organise, 1948
C. 111 and R. 111: Discrimination (Employment and Occupation), 1958

➜ See also **Discrimination; Fundamental principles and rights at work; Globalization; Human resources development; Maternity protection; Migrant workers; Parental leave; Sexual harassment; Social security; Social protection**

F

Facilities and equipment

All welfare facilities at the workplace, such as healthcare services, catering services, sufficient and adequate lavatories/rest-rooms, and equipment such as office supplies and work-related tools should be freely available to employees on an equal basis. Facilities and equipment should, as far as possible, accommodate the practical and cultural needs of all workers, including women, disabled persons and members of particular religious and cultural groups. Where practicable, provision should be made for breastfeeding under adequate hygienic conditions at or near the workplace.

Information should be disseminated to all employees on an equal basis on the availability of these facilities and equipment.

> R. 102: Welfare Facilities, 1956
> C. 155: Occupational Safety and Health, 1981
> C. 161: Occupational Health Services, 1985
> C. 148: Working Environment (Air Pollution, Noise and Vibration), 1977
> C. 120: Hygiene (Commerce and Offices), 1964
> C. 103: Maternity Protection (Revised) and R. 95: Maternity Protection, 1952
> C. 183 and R. 191: Maternity Protection, 2000

→ See also **Breastfeeding workers; Childcare and family services and facilities; Disabilities, workers with; Hygiene in the workplace; Maternity protection; Occupational safety and health**

Family benefit

Family benefit is an allowance payable to workers who have the responsibility for the maintenance of their dependent children (including adopted children). It should be a periodical payment granted to any protected person, irrespective of sex, who has completed the prescribed qualifying period. Recommendation No. 165 (Para. 27) highlights the right to social security benefits for parents, stating that social security benefits, tax relief or other appropriate measures consistent with national policy should, when necessary, be available to workers with family responsibilities.

C. 102: Social Security (Minimum Standards), 1952
C. 118: Equality of Treatment (Social Security), 1962
R. 165: Workers with Family Responsibilities, 1981

➜   See also **Family responsibilities, workers with**

Family responsibilities, workers with

Convention No. 156 defines workers with family responsibilities as men and women workers with responsibilities in relation to their dependent children and other members of their immediate family who clearly need their care or support, where such responsibilities restrict their possibilities of preparing for, entering, participating in or advancing in economic activity (Articles 1-2). It is the responsibility of each member State to determine which persons would be covered by these terms.

All workers, both men and women, should be able to engage in employment without being subject to discrimination related to a perceived conflict between their employment and their family responsibilities. They should be free from restrictions based on family responsibilities when preparing for and entering, participating in or advancing in economic activity.

Convention No. 156 and its accompanying Recommendation No. 165 firmly place equality of opportunity and treatment for workers with family responsibilities within the wider framework of measures to promote equality between the sexes. The principles and objectives to be pursued for the benefit of workers with family responsibilities should therefore, as far as possible, form part of or be closely linked to relevant national policies on equality of opportunity and treatment for male and female workers.

National policies to address this issue in accordance with Convention No. 156 should aim at creating effective equality of opportunity and treatment for female and male workers, and for workers with and without family responsibilities. Such policies should apply equally to wage-earning and non-wage-earning workers. To limit the substantive provisions of the Convention to wage-earners alone would exclude many other workers with family responsibilities, and particularly the self-employed, who constitute a large proportion of the economically active population in most developing countries.

The needs of workers with family responsibilities should particularly be taken into account when planning and developing or promoting community services such as childcare, elder care and family services and facilities. Public information and awareness-raising programmes should be carried out on the situation of these workers. Flexibility in working conditions and in social security should be promoted through:

- the progressive reduction of hours of work and the reduction of the amount of required overtime;

- the introduction of flexible arrangements in working schedules, rest periods and holidays;

- consideration of the place of employment of the spouse and the educational possibilities for children in the case of transfer from one locality to another;

- the regulation and supervision of terms and conditions of employment of part-time workers, workers on temporary contracts and homeworkers: all terms and conditions of employment, including social security should be equivalent to those of full-time and permanent workers;

- consideration of family responsibilities as a valid reason for refusal of an offer of employment (for the purpose of avoiding the loss or suspension of unemployment benefits).

  C. 156 and R. 165: Workers with Family Responsibilities, 1981
  C. 158 and R. 166: Termination of Employment, 1982

➜ See also **Childcare and family services and facilities; Illness in the family, leave for; Marital status; Parental leave; Work–family balance**

Family services and facilities

➜ See **Childcare and family services and facilities**

Female-headed households

Female-headed households are households where either no adult males are present, owing to divorce, separation, migration, non-marriage, or widowhood; or where the men, although present, do not contribute to the household income, because of illness or disability, old age, alcoholism or similar incapacity (but not because of unemployment).

In many countries today, the income generated by women is vital for family survival. Women provide the main source of income in millions of households worldwide – a challenge to the traditional assumption that "head of household" is a role to be occupied by a man. This new reality has to be taken into consideration in modifying, in particular, social security provisions (on pensions, unemployment benefits and family allowances) to ensure that the needs of this group are met, for instance by the further extension of personal social security rights to women. [12] The concept of female-headed households should also be included routinely in national labour statistics to allow the numbers and proportions of this type of household to be clearly identified.

To a larger extent than households headed by men, female-headed households run the risk of poverty because they have less access to well-paid jobs, assets and credit. Their sole responsibility for household work leaves women household heads little or no time to engage in active trade union membership, further education or vocational training. The lack of an enabling environment such as sufficient childcare facilities is therefore also an important factor.

> *C. 156 and R. 165: Workers with Family Responsibilities, 1981*
> *C. 160 and R. 170: Labour Statistics, 1985*

➔ See also **Agricultural and other rural workers; Division of labour; Housework; Informal economy; Labour statistics; Social protection; Social security; Women entrepreneurs**

Flexibility of labour

The flexibility of a labour market is determined by its ability to adapt quickly to new conditions. It occurs in several dimensions of a labour market, including adapting the quantity of labour by means of hiring and firing or recurring to temporary contracts (external flexibility) or by variation in working time, the way work is organized, and the adjustment of wages to respond to shocks and other developments (internal flexibility). Flexible forms of work and casualization, including fixed-term and short-term contracts, agency work, project work, multiple jobs, self-employment and so on, are often associated with insecurity in access to, or coverage by, social security schemes, including pensions, health care and other forms of social assistance. In particular, flexibility is problematic when it takes the form of low-waged work with poor working conditions or is regarded as inevitably involving deregulation. In addition to low levels of security, flexibilized labour markets are also associated with less advantageous contractual/employer-provided legal rights, benefits and working conditions.

---

[12] Personal right is the term used to describe the right of an individual to social benefits in his or her own name. This right may stem from the person's own occupational activity or from the fact that he or she resides in a given country. It is independent of marital status or family situation, except that in some cases benefits may be increased when there are dependants. Derived right is the right of an individual to receive a social benefit by reason of his or her dependence, real or presumed, on a person who is covered by social insurance. This right usually depends on the individual's marital status, which is often taken as proof of the existence or absence of such dependence. Derived rights allow a dependent spouse to benefit from health protection (benefits in kind) and an old-age pension, in the form of survivors' benefits (lump-sum payment or pension) (ILO–EUROPE, 2000, p. 6).

One of the characteristics of labour flexibilization is the greatly increased presence of women in the workforce as part-time workers, workers on non-permanent contracts, homeworkers, remote workers or teleworkers, and in the informal economy. However, not all aspects of flexibility are equally favourable to women. Time flexibility, for instance, does not automatically translate into more attractive employment for parents if it is controlled solely by the employer. Also, while flexibilization has opened up labour markets to women, these opportunities are not necessarily accompanied by labour security. Trade unions also have less capacity to offer adequate representation and possibilities for collective action to women (and men) working outside the structures of formal, full-time employment.

In order to achieve security while providing flexibility, member states should develop or strengthen labour market policies that protect workers during the transition from one job to the next, such as unemployment insurance, active labour market policies and social assistance systems. At the same time, job creation should be promoted by means of employer-friendly tax systems and specific needs should be targeted by gender budgeting.

Most importantly, flexible and short-term contracts should not lead to increased discrimination in employment or be offered as a way of avoiding employers' responsibilities for social protection and equality of opportunity, treatment and remuneration. Measures should be taken to ensure that part-time, temporary and other flexibly employed workers benefit from rights on a pro-rata basis, equivalent to those of permanent, full-time workers, irrespective of sex.

The term "flexicurity" has been coined to express the increasingly important relationship between labour market flexibility and employment security. As a policy-level strategy, flexicurity aims to reconcile the growing flexibilization of labour markets in response to the imperatives of globalization with reasonable employment security and social security, especially for more vulnerable groups of workers. The gender dimension of flexicurity is very important since women's participation in the labour market throughout the life-cycle is different from that of men, tending to be less straightforward and unbroken. One important area of flexicurity with a strong gender dimension is the development of social rights such as maternity and parental leaves, which allow temporary absence from the labour market (flexibility) but guarantee return (security).This concept proves to be a useful approach to the management of labour market changes in Western Europe, but applies also to post-transition countries in Eastern and Central Europe.

R. 198: Employment Relationship, 2006

→ See also **Atypical work; Casual work; Employment relationship; Home work; Part-time work; Social security**

Forced labour

Forced labour may be defined as work or service that is exacted under the menace of a penalty (including non-payment of wages, dismissal from employment, and outright violence or threats of violence) and is undertaken involuntarily (ILO, 2005b, p. 5). It is a severe violation of human rights and restriction of human freedom. Bonded labour (or debt bondage) is a specific form of forced labour in which workers, sometimes their entire families, are obliged to work for an employer or labour contractor in order to pay off loans, wage advances or other obligations, and as a result receive minimal or no payment and lose their freedom to move or change employer. It is particularly prevalent in some South Asian and Latin American countries (but is not confined to them).

As of 2005, the ILO's global estimate of the total number of men, women and children enduring forced labour, in the sense of ILO Conventions Nos. 29 and 105 on forced labour, is a minimum of 12.3 million. Economic activities in which people are forced to work include agriculture, domestic service, sexual exploitation and construction. Bonded labour covers a very broad spectrum of activities including, as well as agriculture, labour in brick kilns and stone quarries, carpet-making, the match and firework industry, and craft work in silver, brass and gems. About 56 per cent of those in forced economic exploitation are women and girls; in forced commercial sexual exploitation the proportion is 98 per cent (ILO, 2005b, p. 15). Disturbing new forms of forced labour such as human trafficking and the abduction and conscription of children into either government-supported or insurgent armies have emerged alongside older forms such as debt bondage (ILO, 2001b). Some four-fifths of forced labour today is exacted by private agents rather than directly by States, although there are still a few States, most notably Burma, which exact forced labour for their own purposes.

Some of the ways in which people become victims of contemporary forced labour are:

•   birth or descent into slave or bonded status;

•   physical abduction or sale of a person;

•   physical confinement in the work location;

•   induced indebtedness by falsification of accounts, unpayable debts contracted with illegal recruitment or migration agents, under- or non-payment of wages, overcharging for food and accommodation, and other means;

•   deceit over the nature and conditions of work promised to migrant workers;

•   threats of violence (including sexual violence) or other sanctions against forced workers and/or their families either at the place of work or in the home country or region of the worker;

- retention of identity documents and threats of denunciation to the authorities, which make irregular migrant workers particularly vulnerable to
coercion.

Women and children are particularly vulnerable to forced labour through trafficking for labour or sexual exploitation, [13] but also through debt bondage, where
women and children are most often bonded through the male household head.
However, there is some evidence of increasing direct bondage of women,
although they may not necessarily have entered into the debt of their own free
will. [14] Older kinds of forced labour are evolving to encompass new labour sectors and new population groups, particularly women and migrant workers.
Forced domestic work is a particular problem area affecting primarily women
and girls; migrant domestic workers – mostly women – can be required to hand
over their identity documents to the household employing them and are then
vulnerable to forced labour. Labour legislation rarely applies effectively to the
domestic work sector.

Forced commercial sexual exploitation represents 11 per cent of all cases worldwide, and is the dominant form of forced labour in transition economies (46 per
cent) and industrialized countries (55 per cent).

Forced and bonded labour are also closely intertwined with child labour (see
p. 36); approximately 40 to 50 per cent of forced labour victims are children
under the age of 18 (ILO, 2005b, p. 15, para. 61).

Forced labour must be treated as a serious crime. As clearly established in
Convention No. 29, the illegal exaction of forced labour shall be punishable as
a penal offence, and it shall be an obligation on any member ratifying the
Convention to ensure that the penalties imposed by law are adequate and
strictly enforced. However, forced labour is infrequently prosecuted, partly
because of difficulty in articulating the offences that constitute forced labour in
national laws and regulations, partly because it is clandestine and invisible. The
line dividing forced labour in the strict legal sense from extremely poor working conditions is sometimes very fine.

It is also important to address forced labour as a distortion of the labour market, and to design labour market regulations and policies on migration in such
a way as to reduce the risk of workers becoming trapped in forced labour
situations. Forced labour is often the result of very long-standing patterns of
discrimination, including discrimination against women. An integrated strategy
that combines rigorous law enforcement with prevention and rehabilitation
measures in a rights-based approach is necessary.

---

[13] The global movement against trafficking has undoubtedly given an impetus to the understanding of
forced labour and action against it; but forced labour is not coextensive with trafficking.

[14] For more on the gender aspects of bonded labour, see *A global alliance against forced labour*, p. 32, box 2.1.

C. 29: Forced Labour, 1930, and R. 35: Forced Labour (Indirect Compulsion), 1930
C. 105: Abolition of Forced Labour, 1957
C. 169: Indigenous and Tribal Peoples, 1989
C. 182 and R. 190: Worst Forms of Child Labour, 1999
Declaration on Fundamental Principles and Rights at Work, 1998

➜   See also **Child labour; Commercial sexual exploitation; Migrant workers; Trafficking in persons**

Freedom of association and the right to organize

Freedom of association and the right to organize are fundamental principles aiming at the free exercise of the right of workers and employers, without any distinction, to associate for the purpose of furthering and defending their interests.

Workers and employers have the right to establish and join organizations of their own choosing. Such organizations must have the right:

*   to draw up their own constitutions and rules;

*   to elect their representatives in full freedom;

*   to organize their administration and activities, and formulate their pro-grammes;

*   not to be dissolved or suspended by administrative authority;

*   to form and join federations and confederations.

Workers should be protected from anti-union discrimination. In particular, they should be protected against refusal to employ them because of their union membership or participation in trade union activities. Also, workers' and employers' organizations should enjoy protection against acts of interference by each other that are designed to promote domination, financing or control.

Throughout the years, many trade unions have been instrumental in supporting and defending the rights of women workers. It is of major importance for the promotion of gender equality that trade unions actively organize women workers and defend their interests adequately through collective bargaining. It is also important for women's representation and voice in trade unions to be increased and for trade unions to become more woman- or family-friendly.

In recent years, discussion about freedom of association has shifted from whether these rights and principles should be respected to how best to respect and use them without discrimination. However, many national laws on freedom of association still exclude from legal protection workers in agriculture, EPZs and the informal economy, migrant workers, and domestic workers – all sectors in which women form a large proportion of workers.

C. 87: Freedom of Association and Protection of the Right to Organise, 1948
C. 98: Right to Organise and Collective Bargaining, 1949
C. 141 and R. 149: Rural Workers' Organisations, 1975
C. 151 and R. 159: Labour Relations (Public Service), 1978
ILO Declaration on Fundamental Principles and Rights at Work
and its Follow-up, 1998

➜ See also **Collective bargaining; Employers' organizations; Fundamental principles and rights at work; Representation and voice; Trade unions; Workers' organizations**

Fundamental principles and rights at work

The fundamental principles and rights of employers and workers are derived from the ILO Constitution and the Declaration of Philadelphia. These principles and rights concern:

• freedom of association and effective recognition of the right to collective bargaining;

• the elimination of forced or compulsory labour;

• the abolition of child labour;

• the elimination of discrimination with respect to employment and occupation.

The fundamental principles and rights are laid down in eight fundamental Conventions (which means that the member States that ratify them thereby commit themselves to putting their provisions into effect in both law and practice):

• freedom of association and the right to collective bargaining: Freedom of Association and Protection of the Right to Organise Convention, 1948 (No. 87) and Right to Organise and Collective Bargaining Convention, 1949 (No. 98).

• elimination of forced or compulsory labour: Forced Labour Convention, 1930 (No. 29) and Abolition of Forced Labour Convention, 1957 (No. 105).

- abolition of child labour: Minimum Age Convention, 1973 (No. 138) and Worst Forms of Child Labour Convention, 1999 (No. 182).

- elimination of discrimination in respect of employment and occupation: Equal Remuneration Convention, 1951 (No. 100) and Discrimination (Employment and Occupation) Convention, 1958 (No. 111).

In 1998, the Declaration on Fundamental Principles and Rights at Work and its Follow-up was adopted by the International Labour Conference. The Declaration is a promotional instrument, intended to reaffirm the commitment of all ILO member States to the fundamental principles and rights to which all countries must adhere by the very fact of their membership of the Organization, even if they have not yet been able to ratify the corresponding Conventions.

All the fundamental principles and rights and fundamental Conventions are of vital interest to women workers, but those protecting rights to non-discrimination are most directly applicable to the promotion of equality between male and female workers. Under the Declaration, the principle of elimination of discrimination in employment and occupation, which covers equal remuneration for work of equal value, and equal opportunity and treatment, is to be respected, realized and promoted in all member States of the ILO.

The follow-up to the Declaration consists of three parts: annual reports by the member States that have not ratified the relevant Conventions; global reports prepared by the ILO each year over a four-year cycle on one of the four categories listed above; and, on the basis of discussion of the global reports in the International Labour Conference, the identification by the ILO Governing Body of priorities for technical cooperation to assist member States in implementing the principles and rights in the Declaration.

The ILO has a special programme dedicated to the promotion of the Declaration, which provides technical cooperation support, gives technical advice to member States, ensures the production of annual and global reports, publishes other reports and research, and organizes relevant seminars, round-tables and capacity-building programmes for ILO constituents and others.

ILO Declaration on Fundamental Principles and Rights at Work and its Follow-up, 1998

G

Gender[15]

Gender refers to the socially constructed differences and relations between males and females. These vary widely among societies and cultures and change over time. The term "gender" is not interchangeable with the term "sex", which refers exclusively to the biological differences between men and women, which are universal and do not change. Statistical data are disaggregated according to sex, whereas gender characterizes the differing roles, responsibilities, constraints, opportunities and needs of females and males in all areas and in any given social context.

Gender roles are learned behaviours in a given society, community or other social group. They condition which activities, tasks and responsibilities are perceived as appropriate to males and females respectively. Gender roles are affected by age, socio-economic class, race/ethnicity, religion, and the geographical, economic, political and cultural environment. Gender relations are also relations of power which affect who can access and control tangible and intangible resources.

Changes in gender roles often occur in response to changing economic, natural or political circumstances including development efforts or structural adjustment, or other nationally or internationally based forces. The gender roles within a given social context may be flexible or rigid, similar or different, and complementary or conflicting. Both women and men are involved to differing degrees and in different ways in reproductive, productive and community management activities and play roles within social and political groups. Their involvement in each activity reflects the gender division of labour in a particular place at a particular time. The gender division of labour must be reflected in gender analysis.

Gender relations have an effect on every aspect of employment, working conditions, social protection, representation and voice at work; this is why gender is called a cross-cutting issue in the world of work. The disparity in any area between women and men in terms of their levels of participation, access to

---

[15] This and the following entries are an interlinked group of conceptual topics relating to gender. They have therefore not been cross-referenced to one another, and the cross-references that appear at the end of each entry are to other topics.

resources, rights, power and influence, remuneration or benefits is often called the gender gap. Of particular relevance to gender equality at work is the gender pay gap, the disparity between the average earnings of men and women; but gender gaps are also evident in access to employment, education and vocational training, and meaningful participation in representative social dialogue institutions.

→   See also **Access to employment; Division of labour; Equal remuneration; Education; Glass ceiling; Vocational training**

Gender analysis and planning

Gender analysis is a tool to diagnose the differences between women and men regarding their specific activities, conditions, needs, access to and control over resources, and their access to development benefits and decision-making. It studies the links between these and other factors in the larger social, economic, political and environmental context.

Gender analysis is the first step in gender-sensitive strategic and development planning. It entails:

*   collecting sex-disaggregated data and gender-sensitive information about the population being addressed;

*   identifying the sexual division of labour, and access to and control over resources and benefits by men and women respectively;

*   understanding girls', boys', women's and men's needs, constraints and opportunities;

*   identifying constraints and opportunities in the larger context;

*   reviewing the capacities of the relevant organizations to promote gender equality.

Gender analysis springs from the concept of "gender and development" (GAD), which itself emerged in the 1980s as a response to criticisms of the "women in development" (WID) approach, began in the early 1970s as researchers started to analyse the sexual division of labour and the specific impact of development on women. The WID approach advocated integrating women into ongoing development strategies, focusing on the disadvantaged position of women and the elimination of discrimination against them. The GAD approach, by contrast, focuses not solely on women but on the social differences and unequal relations between men and women. It emphasizes the contribution of both women and men to shaping gender-equitable development.

Women's empowerment is a concept often used in gender analysis and planning. It generally refers to the idea that the redistribution of unequal power relations between men and women can be advanced by women increasing their self-reliance and internal strength through a process of awareness and capacity building leading to greater participation, greater decision-making power and control, and ultimately to transformative action. Women's economic empowerment means transcending the low-paid and part-time work which often merely serve to reinforce existing gender inequalities. More broadly, meaningful participation in formal decision-making structures (such as governments, employers' organizations and trade unions) is seen as a key aspect of women's empowerment (OECD, 1998). A masculinities focus is also a useful way of looking at changing gender relations by looking at the roles of men and boys. Among other things, it can help increase awareness and acceptance of caring roles for men.

Gender planning may be broadly defined as planning that integrates gender equality and women's empowerment considerations at all stages into the design, implementation, monitoring and evaluation of a programme or project, including the setting of goals and objectives, the definition of strategies and indicators, the selection of methodologies and tools for integrating a gender perspective, gender-related activities and the allocation of resources to carry them out.

Several gender planning approaches and frameworks have been developed, of which the Harvard and Moser frameworks are among the most widely used. For sources of further information on gender planning frameworks, see *Further resources* (p. 206).

→ See also **Division of labour; Labour statistics; Masculinities; Representation and voice**

Gender and development

→ See **Gender analysis and planning**

Gender equality

Gender equality refers to the enjoyment of equal rights, opportunities and treatment by men and women and by boys and girls in all spheres of life. It asserts that people's rights, responsibilities, social status and access to resources do not depend on whether they are born male or female. It does not mean, however, that men and women are the same or must become the same, or that all labour market measures must arrive at the same results. Gender equality implies that all men and women are free to develop their personal abilities and make life choices without the limitations set by stereotypes or prejudices about gender roles or the characteristics of men and women.

In the context of decent work, gender equality embraces equality of opportunity and treatment, equality of remuneration and access to safe and healthy working environments, equality in association and collective bargaining, equality in obtaining meaningful career development, maternity protection, and a balance between work and home life that is fair to both men and women. The ILO understands gender equality as a matter of human rights, social justice and sustainable development.

➜   See also **Decent work; Discrimination; Equal remuneration; Equality of opportunity and treatment in employment; Family responsibilities, workers with; Maternity protection; Millennium Development Goals; Representation and voice**

Gender equity

Gender equity means fairness of treatment for women and men, according to their respective needs and interests. This may include equal treatment or treatment that is different but considered equivalent in terms of rights, benefits, obligations and opportunities.

Gender mainstreaming

Although the concept of gender mainstreaming had been in existence for some years previously, the adoption of gender mainstreaming as the main global strategy for promoting gender equality was clearly established in 1995 at the Fourth World Conference on Women in Beijing. Gender mainstreaming is defined as:

> the process of assessing the implications for women and men of any planned action, including legislation, policies or programmes in any area and at all levels. It is a strategy for making women's as well as men's concerns and experiences an integral dimension of the design, implementation, monitoring and evaluation of policies and programmes in all political, economic and societal spheres so that women and men benefit equally and inequality is not perpetuated. The ultimate goal is to achieve gender equality. (ECOSOC, 1997).

Gender mainstreaming is not a goal in itself, but a means to achieve gender equality. Gender mainstreaming and special interventions to promote equality between women and men are complementary strategies. Special interventions to promote gender equality can target either women alone, both women and men, or men alone. There is no conflict between the two strategies; on the contrary, targeted interventions are seen as essential for mainstreaming.

Using a mainstreaming strategy based on gender analysis implies, in particular:

- awareness-raising and capacity-building activities;

- at the planning, taking into account implementation, monitoring and evaluation stages, the effects of policies and programmes on women and men;

- adequate allocation of human and financial resources;

- active participation of both women and men in decision-making in all areas and at all levels;

- adequate monitoring tools and mechanisms to enable ongoing assessment of how and to what extent gender is being effectively mainstreamed.

There has been a progressive shift from focusing exclusively on women workers of different kinds towards gender mainstreaming as a strategy to counter sex discrimination (see Introduction, section 5). Mainstreaming gender equality in the world of work is a means of integrating equality concerns across the board into all policy objectives and all activities in order to promote equality of all workers, irrespective of sex. The main areas of concern are the following:

- promoting and realizing fundamental principles and rights at work to ensure that the principle of non-discrimination is fully applied in law and in practice;

- creating greater opportunities for women and men to secure decent employment and income, thus achieving the goals of decent living standards, social and economic integration, personal fulfilment and social development;

- enhancing the coverage and effectiveness of social protection for all in order to improve the socio-economic security of all people, including measures to safeguard working conditions and safety and health, and to extend social protection; and

- strengthening tripartism and social dialogue to ensure women's and men's equal participation so that their interests and concerns are adequately reflected in policy-making and implementation.

Girl child labourers

→ See **Child labour**

Glass ceiling

Invisible and artificial barriers that militate against women's access to top decision-making and managerial positions, arising chiefly from a persistent masculine bias in organizational culture, are popularly known as the "glass ceiling".
Although a few women have made it to the very top in the world of work, this
phenomenon is still very prevalent in all but a handful of countries despite
women's increased levels of qualifications, employability and work performance. The glass ceiling has proved resistant to affirmative action, sensitization
of senior managers and human resources staff, measures to promote
work–family balance and a broad recognition that investing in the talents and
qualities of both women and men at all organizational levels makes good business sense.

The existence of the glass ceiling is a prime example of discrimination against
women at work through vertical segregation by sex. It exists because:

- women's career paths tend to be more circuitous and interrupted than
  those of men which are typically linear, and this impedes women's progress to top positions;

- top posts tend to be characterized by masculine values of aggressiveness,
  and suitability for them is decided mostly according to male criteria;

- women are primarily placed in non-strategic sectors rather than in the so-
  called "line" positions that involve financial decision-making or revenue-
  generating responsibilities, positions that are critical for advancement to
  the top;

- women have less access to training and career development activities;

- women workers still bear more of the main burden of family responsibilities than men and so have less time for the "extracurricular" formal and
  informal networking essential for advancement in enterprises.

Clearly, eliminating sex discrimination by law will naturally weaken the glass
ceiling; but the following specific practical strategies may also help:

- enhancing senior managers' awareness of obligations and rights related to
  gender equality;

- affirmative action, mentoring and monitoring for women;

- placing more women in strategic sectors and positions that provide them
  with good career prospects;

- increasing and refining work–family balance measures to enable both
  parents to combine family and career more harmoniously;

- improving women's access to training, in particular in technical and management fields and in business skills and enterprise development to help them run their own businesses;

- fostering the creation of women's formal and informal work- and business-related networks;

- reviewing human resource development practices so as to recognize the potential value of non-conventional career paths and facilitate women's access to managerial positions;

- sensitizing policy-makers and employers to gender equality issues so that they contribute to creating a gender-equitable organizational culture and socio-economic environment.

The metaphor of the glass ceiling has been extended to apply to other areas of vertical and horizontal occupational segregation, such as "glass walls" (concentration of women in certain sectors, women unable to jump the gap between secretarial/administrative and managerial functions regardless of their educational attainments or experience) and the "sticky floor" (women trapped in the lowest-paid jobs or on the bottom rungs of their occupation and unable to rise above the poverty line).

R. 195: Human Resources Development, 2004

➡ See also **Affirmative and positive action; Discrimination; Education; Gender gap; Occupational segregation**

Globalization

Globalization is a complex phenomenon among whose key characteristics are the liberalization of international trade, the expansion of foreign direct investment and the emergence of massive cross-border financial flows, aided by the rapid growth of new technology, especially information and communications technology (ILO, 2004h, p. 24, para. 132).

The impact of globalization and employment restructuring has had important consequences for gender- and equality-related policies worldwide. Investors and multinational companies have enjoyed much greater freedom to move capital from one country to another, thereby creating jobs in countries with lower labour costs and destroying jobs in those with more expensive labour.

Women are often the first to feel both the positive and negative effects because international capital tends to be invested in more labour-intensive production which tends to be female-dominated owing to the lower wages women workers earn in these sectors. In the process of globalization, female participation in paid employment has increased considerably; but this has not led everywhere to women's benefiting equally from their integration into the labour market which remains highly sex-segregated. In many developing countries, deeply embedded gender inequalities mean that the social cost of globalization weighs disproportionately on women. In agriculture, trade liberalization has destroyed the livelihoods of many women farmers or displaced them from their land, while throwing up big obstacles to their entry into the new economic activities generated by globalization. Women have also been hit harder by the financial crises in many countries resulting from globalization (ILO, 2004h, pp. 47–8, paras 214–17).

Many countries have responded to this economic process with legislative and administrative changes, in order to liberalize national labour standards and working conditions and to make them more flexible. The negative effects of globalization are very serious, and there is growing concern internationally that economic globalization must be accompanied by a set of minimum standards in the social field. A particularly grave concern is whether current patterns of globalization are creating, or contributing to, new forms of forced labour such as trafficking in persons for labour exploitation. The tendency to level down social and labour standards in the process of globalization needs to be tackled. Political, business and trade union leaders must accept their shared responsibility and pay attention to international labour standards, thus contributing to improving working conditions for both women and men.

→ See also **Atypical work; Export-processing zones; Flexibility of labour; Fundamental principles and rights at work; Informal economy; Labour market; Migrant workers; Social protection; Trafficking in persons**

Grievance procedures

Any worker who, acting individually or jointly with others, considers that she or he has grounds to complain about treatment in employment should have the right to submit a grievance and have it dealt with through appropriate procedures without suffering any prejudice whatsoever.

Within the workplace, procedures for examining grievances based on discriminatory employment practices and treatment should be established, and should be accessible and operational for all workers. Some grievance procedures begin with informal or formal conciliation in order to help the parties find a solution. Comprehensive grievance procedures should be developed and implemented in the workplace by the employer and the workers or their representatives. The procedures should include the following:

- a committee (containing both men and women) composed of representatives of employees and management to supervise the system, review complaints, collect relevant information, make appropriate factual inquiries, decide on the outcome and implement decisions;

- a procedure and an explanation for the filing of complaints of discriminatory practices which are made known to all employees and job applicants;

- the basis, which must not be restricted to the identification of one particular group or sex, upon which a complaint of discrimination may be filed;

- a standard, swift, free and fair procedure, based upon objective criteria, to evaluate and resolve complaints;

- a set of effective sanctions and accompanying enforcement procedures to be applied to those who are responsible for discriminatory practices and treatment.

Procedures for dealing with complaints should be impartial and should enable the matter to be settled quickly. Employees should be informed of the grievance procedures and should be encouraged to complain against discriminatory practices. Appeal procedures into the formal labour disputes settlement regime should also be available. Full weight should be attached to the need for confidentiality.

R. 92: Voluntary Conciliation and Arbitration, 1951
R. 130: Examination of Grievances, 1967

➜ See also **Disciplinary action; Harassment and pressure; Remedies and sanctions; Sexual harassment**

H

Harassment and pressure

Harassment and pressure (also known as bullying or mobbing) at the workplace can occur as various offensive behaviours. It is characterized by persistently negative attacks of a physical or psychological nature, which are typically unpredictable, irrational and unfair, on an individual or group of employees. Sexual harassment is a particular form of harassment.

Electronic surveillance of workers also has the potential to constitute harassment in some circumstances.

No worker, female or male, should be subjected to harassment or pressure in any term or condition of employment, or to any emotional abuse, persecution or victimization at work. In particular, there should be no sexual harassment. Work assignments should be distributed equally and based on objective criteria. The job performances of all employees should be evaluated objectively. Employees should not encounter obstacles in the performance of their job functions and should not be required to perform additional work duties or assignments on the basis of their sex. Victims of harassment and pressure should be protected from retaliatory or disciplinary action by adequate preventive measures and means of redress.

There is growing awareness that harassment and pressure at the workplace is not merely an individual human problem but is rooted in the wider social, economic, organizational and cultural context, which includes pervasive inequalities in gender relations. As research indicates, the effects of harassment are also a costly burden for the worker, the enterprise and the community. Harassment should therefore be addressed by adequate measures.

The ILO's TRAVAIL department has a special programme on workplace violence and harassment, concerned with the prevention of all forms of workplace violence including bullying, mobbing, and harassment on grounds such as sex, race or ethnicity, religion, or sexual orientation. The programme conducts and commissions research into these issues, develops practical tools and offers advice to governments and workers' and employers' organizations on how to prevent and respond to harassment.

C. 111 and R. 111: Discrimination (Employment and Occupation), 1958
C. 169: Indigenous and Tribal Peoples, 1989

→   See also **Computers; Grievance procedures; Sexual harassment; Violence at work**

Health during maternity

ILO Conventions and Recommendations for the protection of pregnant and nursing women workers all make provision for the protection of such workers' health during maternity. The general principle is stated in Maternity Protection Convention, 2000 (No. 183), which states:

Each Member shall, after consulting the representative organizations of employers and workers, adopt appropriate measures to ensure that pregnant or breastfeeding women are not obliged to perform work which has been determined by the competent authority to be prejudicial to the health of the mother or the child, or where an assessment has established a significant risk to the mother's health or that of her child. (ILO, 2000, Art. 3)

The Maternity Protection Recommendation, 1952 (No. 95) states that night work and overtime work should be prohibited for pregnant and nursing women. During pregnancy and up to at least three months after confinement, women should not be employed on work prejudicial to their health or that of the child. In particular, the employment of pregnant and nursing women is prohibited with regard to:

- any hard labour involving lifting heavy weights, pulling or pushing or undue physical strain, including prolonged standing;

- work requiring special balance;

- work with vibrating machines.

Recommendation No. 191 on maternity protection states that measures should be taken to provide, on the basis of a medical certificate as appropriate, alternatives to work defined as harmful to the health of a pregnant or nursing woman or her child. These may include adaptation of the woman's conditions of work; transfer to another post not harmful to her health without loss of pay when such an adaptation is not feasible; or paid leave in accordance with national laws, regulations or practice when such a transfer is not feasible.

Special precautions or alternative employment may be necessary in the case of pregnant women working in the presence of radiation.

C. 103: Maternity Protection (Revised) and R95: Maternity Protection, 1952
C. 183 and R. 191: Maternity Protection, 2000
P. 89: Protocol of 1990 to the Night Work (Women) (Revised), 1948
C. 171: Night Work, 1990
C. 102: Social Security (Minimum Standards), 1952
R. 116: Reduction of Hours of Work, 1962
R. 114: Radiation Protection, 1960

C. 110: Plantations, 1958 (and Protocol, 1982)
R. 157: Nursing Personnel, 1977
C. 170 and R. 177: Chemicals, 1990

➜ See also **Breastfeeding workers; Chemicals; Maternity protection; Night work; Radiation protection**

Health insurance

A health insurance scheme is a public or private scheme for the reimbursement of medical or hospital care or compensation for loss of income due to illness, injury or accident. A health insurance system should be compulsory for all workers, with the following exemptions:

• temporary and occasional employment;

• cases where wages or income exceed the amount determined by national law;

• cases where the remuneration is not a money wage;

• workers below or above age limits established by the law;

• members of the employer's family.

Health insurance should be available equally to men and women, although there will be differences depending on whether a worker is in full-time or part-time employment. Compulsory health insurance schemes are not applicable in many spheres of work in which women predominate (self-employment, the informal economy, etc.), so they are obliged to take personal responsibility for this protection.

The system should be administered by non-profit institutions under the supervision of the competent public authority. The insured persons and the employers should share the financial burden of the system. In case of incapacity for work on health grounds, the insured person is entitled to receive:

• a cash benefit for at least the first 26 weeks of incapacity for work;

• medical treatment, medicines and appliances free of charge or on paying only a part of the cost.

Among relevant standards, Recommendation No. 29 on sickness insurance in 1927, though of outdated status, is the only ILO occupational safety and health instrument to specifically mention discrimination on the grounds of sex.

> *R. 29: Sickness Insurance, 1927*
> *C. 102: Social Security (Minimum Standards), 1952*
> *C. 130: Medical Care and Sickness Benefits, 1969*

→   See also **Conditions and benefits of employment; Social protection; Social security**

HIV/AIDS

HIV is the English acronym for the Human Immunodeficiency Virus, a virus that weakens the body's immune system and ultimately causes AIDS (Acquired Immune Deficiency Syndrome), a cluster of medical conditions (often referred to as opportunistic infections) and cancers. The virus is incurable to date. HIV/AIDS is a pandemic which has spread with terrifying speed throughout the world, and as such, is a workplace issue and should be treated like any other serious illness or condition in the workplace (ILO, 2001a, pp. 1, 3).

HIV/AIDS status is one in the group of conditions and attributes recently recognized as prohibited grounds for discrimination in employment or occupation. The ILO has had a particular interest in this issue for some years, because discrimination in the workplace on grounds of HIV status is growing around the world as fast as the HIV pandemic itself, and because accelerating infection rates devastate workers, their families, their workplaces and the whole social fabric.

In 1988 the ILO and the WHO adopted a joint Declaration on HIV/AIDS from the Consultation on AIDS and the Workplace, which contains provisions on discrimination in the workplace. The *ILO Code of Practice on HIV/AIDS in the world of work* was endorsed by a UN Special Session of the General Assembly on the subject in 2001. The code emphasizes the need to fight discrimination against workers with real or perceived HIV positive status or living with AIDS, and discusses the gender dimension of the pandemic (ILO, 2001a, pp. 21–2).

The existing discrimination women face makes them more vulnerable to HIV/AIDS, as is shown by the rising rate of female infection, especially among young women aged 15–24. However, men and boys also face discrimination on the grounds of real or perceived HIV-positive status. Fear and ignorance fuel this discrimination. Co-workers may fear contact with an infected person, while employers view employing HIV-positive people as costly from a care and treatment angle and potentially bad for productivity. Discrimination against people known or suspected to be HIV-positive may take the form of pre-employment testing (which is currently mandatory for foreign workers and students in as many as 60 countries), breach of medical confidentiality leading to the worker's dismissal or resignation, denial of insurance benefits, demotion, pay cuts, and harassment.

While there is no international labour standard that specifically addresses HIV/AIDS in the workplace, a large number of instruments covering both protection against discrimination and prevention of infection can be applied to workplace issues related to HIV/AIDS (Hodges-Aeberhard, 1999).

Those countries with legislation and regulations on this subject consider that a definition of prohibited discrimination based on the HIV status of a worker should be as broad and universal as possible. Such a definition should include discrimination against both symptomatic and asymptomatic persons infected by the virus, as well as that based on the mere suspicion that an individual could be infected because he or she belongs to a so-called high-risk group, or because of his or her relationship with an infected person.

HIV/AIDS also reinforces patterns of gender inequality through its effects on the female members of the families of HIV-positive people, since the burden of caring for persons ill with AIDS-related diseases and also compensating for their loss of income falls largely on them. The more severe the gender discrimination in societies, the more negatively women are affected by HIV. Therefore, more equal gender relations and the empowerment of women are vital to the successful prevention of the spread of HIV infection and enabling women to cope with HIV/AIDS (Hodges-Aeberhard, 1999, p. 3).

Addressing the role of men and boys in promoting gender equality has also become recognized as an important way of helping to prevent the spread of HIV. The ILO held a seminar on this topic in Brasilia in October 2003 (UNDAW, 2003).

C. 98: Right to Organise and Collective Bargaining, 1949
C. 102: Social Security (Minimum Standards), 1952
C. 111 and R. 111: Discrimination (Employment and Occupation), 1958
C. 121: Occupational Injury Benefits, 1964
C. 97: Migration for Employment (Revised), 1949
C. 143: Migrant Workers (Supplementary Provisions), 1975
C. 149: Nursing Personnel, 1977
C. 154: Collective Bargaining, 1981
C. 155 and R. 160: Occupational Safety and Health, 1981
C. 158: Termination of Employment, 1982
C. 159: Vocational Rehabilitation and Employment (Disabled Persons), 1983
C. 161 and R. 171: Occupational Health Services, 1985
C. 175: Part-Time Workers, 1994
C. 182: Worst Forms of Child Labour, 1999
Declaration on Fundamental Principles and Rights at Work, 1998
Joint ILO/WHO Declaration on HIV/AIDS in the Workplace, 1988

➜ See also **Discrimination; Diversity in the workplace; Illness in the family, leave for; Masculinities; Nursing personnel; Social protection**

Home work

Homeworkers are defined in the 1993 International Classification of Status in Employment as those who work for an enterprise to supply goods or services by prior arrangement with that enterprise, and whose place of work is not within any of the enterprise's premises (ILO, 2004a, p. 11 and ILO, 1993a). The difference between a dependent homeworker and an independent own-account worker operating from her or his own home is determined by a wide variety of factors in different legal systems. Recommendation No. 198 on the employment relationship lists a number of these, such as control or periodic payment of remuneration to the person.

Official statistics on home work are scarce, because home-based work has not been recognized as a distinct form of employment in most countries, making homeworkers invisible to national statistics (ILO, 2003, p. 88). However, there is evidence that this form of work is becoming increasingly common, especially among women, and that this growth is facilitated by the growing use of sub-contracting and industrial outsourcing and the rapid spread of information and communications technology. Home-based work is also a strategy for reconciling work and family responsibilities for women.

In some cases, mostly in developed countries, home-based work can be a positive choice for women and can be professional and well-paid (though still poorly protected). Studies indicate, however, that the large majority of homeworkers are low-income, low-skilled women and particularly women with young children (about 90 per cent of the worldwide average), and the entry into home-based work is a survival strategy rather than a career choice. Women with disabilities are also disproportionately represented. While women homeworkers may benefit from independence in their work location and flexibility in hours of work, there are also concerns about the disadvantages associated with home work, which include long hours of work, poor and irregular remuneration, limited access to social security, welfare and similar benefits, safety and health problems, and isolation leading to difficulties in organizing and bargaining effectively.

In most countries, home work is covered by regulations similar to those for any other labour relationship, except as regards working hours and breaks, which are outside the employer's control. However, compliance with regulations is difficult to monitor and enforce through labour inspectorates, and the work is often undeclared by both employers and workers.

The Home Work Convention and Recommendation, 1996 (No. 177 and No. 184) promote equality of treatment between homeworkers and other wage earners. National policies dealing with home-based work should be designed, implemented and periodically reviewed to promote as far as possible equality of treatment between homeworkers and other wage earners and to improve the homeworker's situation, particularly with regard to:

- freedom of association;

- protection against discrimination;

- equal remuneration for work of equal value;

- paid public holidays, annual holidays with pay, and paid sick leave;

- statutory social security protection;

- occupational safety and health;

- minimum age and maternity protection;

- access to vocational training and professional/career development.

  C. 156 and R. 165: Workers with Family Responsibilities, 1981
  C. 177 and R. 184: Home Work, 1996
  R. 198: Employment Relationship, 2006

➜ See also **Atypical work; Care work; Computers; Domestic workers; Family responsibilities, workers with; Remote working; Work-family balance**

Hours of work

Limitation of the hours they work is a central right of workers. In particular, it is a measure of gender equity insofar as limits on working hours allow time for domestic and care work for both women and men. Hours of work has been a key concern of the ILO throughout its history. The limits were initially designated as a 48-hour week and an 8-hour day, in ILO standards such as the Hours of Work (Industry) Convention, 1919 (No. 1) and the Hours of Work (Commerce and Offices) Convention, 1930 (No. 30). The more modern standard is a 40-hour week, enshrined in the Forty-Hour Week Convention, 1935 (No. 47) and the Reduction of Hours of Work Recommendation, 1962 (No. 116).[16]

In cases where reduced duration of the working day or week is being considered, priority should be accorded to industries and professions involving particularly physically or intellectually demanding work and health hazards to workers, especially when the labour force is made up of women and young people.

------

[16] For the incidence of each of these standards around the world, see McCann, 2005.

Pregnant women and breastfeeding mothers should not be required to work overtime and this exemption should imply no prejudice to their career development. Also, the working schedule should be organized to allow pregnant and breastfeeding women sufficient rest periods. Many national laws also designate "rest breaks" for all workers during the working day (e.g. 30 minutes per day).

Long working hours are a particular problem for workers in atypical work situations such as domestic workers, particularly if they are residential, even in countries that have specific labour regulations applying to domestic workers. The working hours of nursing personnel also require careful regulation, and a distinction is made between normal hours of work, overtime, on-call duty (when nursing personnel are, at the workplace or elsewhere, at the disposal of the employer in order to respond to possible calls), and inconvenient hours (hours worked on other than the normal working days and at other than the normal hours of work of the country). On the other hand, for many atypical workers the problem is rather one of insufficient, unpredictable or irregular hours. Labour flexibility tends to translate into work done at "non-standard" times, such as nights (see *Night work,* p. 137) and weekends and also includes irregular schedules.

Shift work has potential negative effects on workers' health and safety, especially where night work is involved. These include disruption of sleep, increased and chronic fatigue, cardiovascular and gastro-intestinal troubles, effects on reproductive health, and increased risk of breast cancer (for women on night shifts). Shift work also disrupts workers' family and social lives and impedes workers' full exercise of the right to organize in trade unions.

All workers irrespective of sex are entitled to a weekly rest (with authorized exceptions) of at least 24 consecutive hours during the days already established by the traditions or customs of the country, and a period of at least three weeks per year of annual paid leave (after a minimum period of service), not counting public and customary holidays (with proportionate paid holiday or compensation to be granted in cases of dismissal). In accordance with the provisions of Convention No. 156, work–family balance policies might mean that in the timetabling of annual paid leave in a workplace, the parents of school-age children are granted priority for leave during school vacations.

> *C. 1: Hours of Work (Industry), 1919*
> *C. 14: Weekly Rest (Industry), 1921*
> *C. 30: Hours of Work (Commerce and Offices), 1930*
> *C. 47: Forty-Hour Week, 1935*
> *C. 101: Holidays with Pay (Agriculture), 1952*
> *C. 106 and R. 103: Weekly Rest (Commerce and Offices), 1957*
> *R. 116: Reduction of Hours of Work, 1962*
> *C. 132: Holidays with Pay (Revised), 1970*

C. 156: Workers with Family Responsibilities, 1981
C. 171 and R. 178: Night Work, 1990

→ See also **Agricultural and other rural workers; Breastfeeding workers; Casual work; Conditions and benefits of employment; Maternity protection; Night work; Nursing personnel; Part-time work; Plantation workers; Family responsibilities, workers with; Work–family balance**

Housework

Housework (as distinct from paid domestic work) is the unremunerated work of maintaining a household which is performed by household members. Women everywhere still bear the primary responsibility for housework. Although the share of housework done by men is rising gradually, principally in developed countries, it is still a small proportion of the total time spent on housework. Even when they have economic responsibilities within and outside the home, women and girls usually have to do the large majority of household tasks by virtue of their assumed customary role in society. This work includes childcare and elder care. It is generally neither regulated nor protected by the law.

In most countries, a housewife has no individual right to a pension, although in some countries it is possible to make voluntary pension contributions. If the housewife is married, she generally has the right to the social benefits of her working husband (revertible pension, family allowances, health assistance). The growing number of female-headed households, in combination with limited access to profitable work and to social security schemes, is a major factor in the "feminization of poverty".

→ See also **Care work; Division of labour; Domestic workers; Economic activity; Elder care; Female-headed households; Social protection; Social security; Unpaid work**

Human resources development

Deep-rooted perceptions regarding the work of men and women have been identified as a major obstacle to achieving gender equality. The development of human resources should tackle these traditional attitudes by raising awareness, investing in women's human capital and thus increasing their employability.

Efforts should be made to inform and influence the general public, as well as parents and employers, on the need to replace traditional attitudes with a new understanding of work and gender equality. It is also essential to develop human resources at the enterprise level involving workers' participation. Appropriate policies and programmes should be developed and implemented in the fields of:

- vocational guidance and vocational training, closely linked with employment;

- training for managers and self-employed persons;

- programmes for particular areas or branches of economic activity and for particular groups of the population;

- the promotion of gender equality in training and employment;

- training for migrant workers;

- training staff in vocational training and vocational guidance, research and administrative aspects, and preparing them to serve on representative bodies.

Vocational training, vocational guidance and continuing learning play a vital role in diversifying the professional choices of women and facilitating their access to better-paid jobs, autonomous work, managerial posts and entrepreneurship.

> *C. 111 and R. 111: Discrimination (Employment and Occupation), 1958*
> *C. 117: Social Policy (Basic Aims and Standards), 1962*
> *C. 140: Paid Educational Leave, 1974*
> *C. 142: Human Resources Development, 1975*
> *R. 195: Human Resources Development, 2004*

➔ See also **Access to employment; Career opportunities; Occupational segregation; Vocational guidance; Vocational training**

Hygiene in the workplace

The following rules concerning hygiene in the workplace should be observed and enforced in all commercial and administrative (public and private) workplaces:

- Workplaces and their equipment should be properly maintained and kept clean.

- The lighting should preferably be natural; artificial light should be appropriately distributed.

- The temperature should be maintained at appropriate levels, and natural or artificial ventilation should be available at all workplaces.

- Sanitary conveniences should be sufficient, suitable and properly maintained. Washing facilities should be provided for workers' use. Separate conveniences and facilities should be provided for men and women except in establishments with no more than five persons or when only the employer's family is employed.

- Rooms should be provided where alternative facilities are not available for temporary rest during working hours, in particular to meet the needs of women workers, for instance for breastfeeding.

- Workers should be protected by appropriate measures against substances, processes and techniques which are unhealthy, toxic or harmful. Special care should be taken in the case of pregnant workers.

C. 120 and R. 120: Hygiene (Commerce and Offices), 1964
C. 148 and R. 156: Working Environment (Air Pollution, Noise
and Vibration), 1977
R. 95: Maternity Protection, 1952 and R. 191: Maternity Protection, 2000

➜ See also **Biological risks; Breastfeeding workers; Chemicals; Facilities and equipment; Occupational health services; Occupational safety and health**

I

Illegal employment

➜ See **Clandestine work**

Illness in the family, leave for

Male and female workers should be entitled to leave in the case of the illness of a dependent member of the immediate family who needs that worker's care or support, or the death of an immediate family member. However, indirect discrimination may occur as a result of the use of this entitlement in practice. As takeup rates of leave provisions are higher for women than men, leave provisions may be perceived as increasing the indirect costs of women's labour, and this may be used to justify offering lower wages in industries where women predominate. Where such leave is not available, it is most probably the mother or daughter who makes the necessary arrangements, with similarly discriminatory consequences, since women are then seen as unreliable workers.

C. 156 and R. 165: Workers with Family Responsibilities, 1981

➜ See also **Elder care; Family responsibilities, workers with; HIV/AIDS; Sick leave**

Indigenous and tribal peoples

Workers who belong to indigenous and tribal peoples have the right to enjoy equal opportunities and equal treatment in employment for women and men. The Indigenous and Tribal Peoples Convention, 1989 (No. 169) stipulates that indigenous and tribal peoples should enjoy, without discrimination, the full measure of human rights and fundamental freedoms. This also implies that cultural practices that undermine indigenous and tribal women's rights should be addressed by the communities concerned. Convention No. 169 is also the only international instrument which explicitly includes protection from sexual harassment (Art. 20.3 (d)).

Governments should develop, with the participation of the peoples concerned, coordinated and systematic action to protect the rights of indigenous and tribal peoples and to guarantee respect for their integrity. Efforts should be made to ensure that they benefit on an equal footing from the rights and opportunities granted to other members of the population, with respect for the social and cultural identity of the peoples in question as well as their customs and institutions. Special measures that are not contrary to their freely expressed wishes should be implemented to safeguard the individuals, institutions, lands, property, labour, cultures and environment of the peoples. The Convention underlines that consultation with, and the participation of, indigenous peoples in processes that affect them are the key principles respecting their rights.

The ILO's work in the field of indigenous and tribal peoples falls into two main categories: the adoption and supervision of standards, and assistance to indigenous and tribal peoples and to States. It also adopted in 1989 a Resolution on indigenous and tribal peoples, to promote the ratification of Convention No. 169.

Women workers who belong to indigenous and tribal peoples are often vulnerable to multiple discrimination. Convention No. 111 is relevant in these cases as well as Convention No. 169.

> *C. 107 and R. 104: Indigenous and Tribal Populations, 1957*
> *C. 169: Indigenous and Tribal Peoples, 1989*
> *C. 111 and R. 111: Discrimination (Employment and Occupation), 1958*

➜ See also **Affirmative action; Discrimination; Diversity; Sexual harassment; Women's entrepreneurship**

Indirect discrimination

➜ See **Discrimination**; see also **Affirmative action; Non-traditional occupations; Occupational segregation**

Informal economy

Although countries work with different definitions of the informal economy, the term may be understood to refer to "all economic activities by workers and economic activities that are – in law or in practice – not covered, or insufficiently covered, by formal arrangements" (ILO, 2002a, para. 3). [17] The term has

---

[17] See "Conclusions concerning decent work and the informal economy", pp. 53–61.

largely replaced "informal sector", perhaps in general acknowledgement of the ever-growing economic weight of informal activities in the international and national economies.

The concept of the informal economy covers two very different situations:

- informality due to the lack of a formal reference point, where there is no applicable labour standard, and thus no obligations to be filled or rights to be respected or demanded;

- informality due to non-conformity with a legal reference point, where applicable labour standards exist but are completely or partially flouted and neither obligations nor rights are recognized.

Informal work covers a very diverse range of models including own-account small businesses, small-scale family enterprises, retail trading, home-based and remote work, Internet-based work, and certain forms of subcontracting. Particularly (but not exclusively) in industrialized countries, it now embraces highly qualified professionals such as information technology specialists, as well as people working in the creative and performing arts. In developing countries, informal self-employment includes unregistered employers, own-account workers and unpaid contributing family workers, and informal waged work covers casual labourers, domestic workers and unregistered employees, among others. Women's unemployment may often be masked or disguised as employment in the informal economy.

The informal economy represents a significant proportion of the economy and labour market in many countries, especially developing ones, and it is growing and diversifying, impelled among other things by the growth of e-commerce and electronically provided services. Profound changes are taking place in the processes which give rise to informal activities, and in the way they operate and fit into national economies. Goods and services produced in the informal sector are no longer only for local consumption in low-income households but also for international markets through subcontracting arrangements with globalized formal-sector enterprises.

In general, work in the informal economy is far less secure and more poorly paid than work in the formal economy, and the influence of the state and of formal labour market institutions is often weak. Workers in the informal economy do not benefit from conventional social protection schemes or legal and regulatory frameworks. In some cases such as EPZs, working conditions are regulated but social security is not. Limited access to resources, information, products, markets, credit, infrastructure, training facilities, technical expertise and improved technologies poses a serious problem for improving the productivity of, and return on, informal labour. In a Resolution concerning decent work and the informal economy adopted at its 90th Session in 2002, the International

Labour Conference recalled that, as a consequence of the feminization of poverty and discrimination by gender, age, ethnicity or disability, the most marginalized groups, including poor women, tend to end up in the informal economy, where decent work deficits are most pronounced.

Women are disproportionately and increasingly represented in the informal economy at all levels. Informal work is an essential source of employment and income for many women workers as an alternative to occupational segregation, unemployment and underemployment. In developing countries, women are mainly engaged in subsistence labour and informal activities linked to the new tradable sectors. Although they usually bear the costs of setting up their informal activity, they do not always control the benefits, which may be appropriated by male relatives.

Workers in the informal economy are protected by a number of ILO Conventions. To begin with, they are covered by all the Conventions which protect fundamental rights and principles at work, and by a number of standards that refer to "workers" rather than "employees" or do not contain language limiting their application to the formal economy (Trebilcock, 2004, p. 590). Many standards, in addition, contain provisions for the extension of application to informal-economy workers.

An appropriate strategy for upgrading the informal economy in a gender-sensitive way should therefore cover:

•   addressing the challenge of guaranteeing fundamental rights for all workers, including issues of equality and non-discrimination;

•   improving productivity, and employment- and income-generating capacity, through access to credit, technology, and training for all informal workers, with particular attention and if necessary special measures for women;

•   establishing a regulatory framework, including appropriate and gender-relevant forms of social protection (e.g. culturally sensitive maternity and work–family balance provisions);

•   encouraging the organization of informal economy workers, especially women;

•   improving welfare systems for the poorest groups in ways that do not add to women's burden of domestic work;

•   continuing to gather statistics and refine analysis of the employment of women and men in the informal economy.

   C. 168: Employment Promotion and Protection against Unemployment, 1988
   R. 169: Employment Policy (Supplementary Provisions), 1984
   C. 177 and R184: Home Work, 1996

R. 189: Job Creation in Small and Medium-Sized Enterprises, 1998
R. 198: Employment Relationship, 2006

➜   See also **Domestic work; Clandestine work; Employment relationship; Home work; Occupational segregation; Self-employed workers**

Inherent/genuine requirements of the job

➜   See **Discrimination**

Invalidity benefit

➜   See **Conditions and benefits of employment;** see also **Employment injury benefit; Social protection; Social security**

J

Job description

A job description lists the essential features of a job, describing the tasks and functions included and the qualifications required for performance.

The job description should be written following an established format and evaluated according to a common, objective standard. This format should, for example, contain elements such as job title, type of supervision received and given, relationships (e.g. line management) within the organization, description of the principal functions of the job and the time required by each function, as well as qualifications such as the education, experience and abilities required.

Job descriptions should be written in gender-sensitive language. Care should be taken that qualifications stated as requisite for the job are not worded in such a way that they apply, directly or indirectly, to one sex only. For instance, if a job involves physical strength, the job description should establish this ability as an objective employment criterion unrelated to the sex of a candidate.

If the organization aspires to be gender-equitable, it should be clearly stated in all job descriptions that the worker will be responsible for mainstreaming gender equality as appropriate within the scope of the job. The ability to carry out basic gender analysis and planning should be included in the job description as a required competency for all professional and managerial staff.

→   See also **Equal remuneration; Job evaluation and classification**

Job evaluation and classification

Job evaluation and classification are elements in a system of comparing different jobs to provide a basis for a grading and a pay structure.

Job classification is a set of categories used to classify jobs in a particular enterprise or organization. In a job classification scheme, individual jobs are graded by reference to benchmark jobs and grade descriptions.

Job evaluation is the logical determination of the relative value of individual jobs in an organization for such purposes as wage determination and promotion.

The aim is to evaluate the job, not the person who is doing the job; in this sense job evaluation should not be confused with performance appraisal (see p. 153), which does evaluate the performance of the person doing the job. The process involves evaluating one job in relation to others by means of a weighting system for the various elements of the jobs compared. Non-discriminatory job evaluation should lead to a payment system within which work of equal value receives equal pay regardless of the sex of the person doing the job.

Job evaluation should be conducted regularly according to a schedule known to all employees and applied equally so that women workers are not subjected to more intense or frequent scrutiny than male workers. The assessment criteria should be objective, related to the functions of the job, and applied on equal terms to all employees. Supervisory staff and employees should be informed about evaluation and appraisal criteria and trained to apply them.

Various types of methodology are used. The analytical job evaluation system compares jobs against preselected objective factors such as skill, effort, responsibility and working conditions. There is growing consensus that this methodology is the most practicable method of ensuring the application of the principle of equal pay for work of equal value.

Work typically done by women is often under-evaluated. Job evaluation criteria should therefore be reviewed and revised to ensure that they do not discriminate directly or indirectly against women workers. The criteria selected should be broad enough to encompass factors that adequately measure the specific aspects of women's and men's work. Care work or teaching, for instance, should not be regarded as inherently less valuable than work requiring physical strength or psychological aggressiveness, qualities stereotypically seen as masculine.

The Resolution on Gender Equality, Pay Equity and Maternity Protection adopted by the ILC in June 2004 calls on employers' and workers' organizations to promote the introduction of gender-neutral job evaluation schemes.

> *C. 100 and R. 90: Equal Remuneration, 1951*
> *C. 111 and R. 111: Discrimination (Employment and Occupation), 1958*

➡ See also **Care work; Equal remuneration; Job description**

L

Labour administration

Labour administration is the institutional framework within which national labour policy is developed, implemented, coordinated, checked and reviewed. National labour policy covers the fields of employment and vocational training, labour protection, industrial relations. research, and labour market information and inspection.

The principal functions of labour administration are to provide for the protection of workers through the preparation, development, adoption, application and review of labour standards, including relevant laws and regulations to promote equality and social justice in the world of work. The protection of workers as regards the improvement of occupational safety and health for both men and women workers is also a fundamental function of labour administration.

The labour administration system should play a vital role in preventing discrimination, making all actors aware of the concept of gender equality, and creating an enabling environment for promoting gender equality. It can do this by making sure women workers' rights and gender equality issues are integrated into:

- the drafting and reviewing of national labour standards;

- assistance offered to workers, employers and their respective organizations in negotiations leading to the adoption of new labour standards through collective bargaining;

- the involvement of the social partners in the preparation and application of standards on working conditions, terms of employment and occupational safety and health;

- the effective application of labour standards through labour inspection;

    C. 150 and R. 158: Labour Administration, 1978

➜ See also **Labour inspection; Public employment services and private employment agencies**

Labour force

The labour force, or economically active population, is defined as the sum of those who are either working (employed) or available for and seeking work (unemployed) at any given moment. The total employed population includes waged and salaried workers (employees), self-employed workers and contributing (unpaid) family workers. The unemployed population comprises all persons of working age who during a recent brief reference period were without work, currently available for work, and actively looking for work. In 2006 women made up 40 per cent of the global labour force (ILO, 2007, pp. 2 and 14).

The labour force participation rate (LFPR) expresses the share of employed plus unemployed persons in comparison with the working-age population, indicating how many people of working age are actively participating in the labour market. LFPR can also be applied to more specific populations such as women, men, or people in particular age bands. Although labour force participation varies considerably between countries and regions, the gap between the rate for men and women has been narrowing in most regions of the world in the last decade, leading to a minimal decrease of the gap at the world level: in 2006, for every 100 economically active men, 67 women were active. Ten years ago, the ratio was 66 women per 100 men (ILO, 2007, pp. 2 and 14). It is important to remember that a high or rising LFPR for women does not necessarily mean that things are improving, since the LFPR per se cannot provide a guide to the likelihood of being employed or to the decency of the work that might be obtained. In this regard, the employment-to-population ratio gives additional information on how many women of working age actually work. Despite the fact that more women are working today than ever before, this ratio is considerably smaller for women than for men in all regions of the world. In 2006, 48.9 per cent of women of working age were in work. For men the ratio was 74.0 per cent.

One striking and related trend has occurred in the labour force since the 1980s: the proliferation of forms of work and employment which differ from the norm of permanent, full-time, socially secure employment, such as part-time work, job sharing, fixed-term contracts, temporary agency work, home work, self-employment, and casual and seasonal work.

At the same time, unemployment now stands at its highest ever, with nearly 195 million economically active people worldwide, some 6 per cent of the global labour force, having no work at all in 2006, and almost half of these being young people aged 15–24. Some 82 million of these unemployed people are women. The unemployment rate is generally higher for women than for men in vulnerably groups such as migrants, young people, and older, disabled and rural workers.

But unemployment is just the tip of the iceberg. Many of the women in the world who work (often under very bad conditions) still belong to the working poor – those people who work but do not earn enough to rise with their families above the US$1-a-day poverty line. Their share is higher than the men's share. Careful estimates show that nearly two-thirds of the 507 million working poor in the world are women (ILO, 2007, p. 13).

→   See also **Atypical work; Economic activity; Female-headed households; Labour statistics; Self-employed workers; Unemployment**

Labour inspection

Labour inspection is a public service whose aim is to supervise compliance with all legal provisions for the protection of workers. It is an indispensable part of national labour administration strategies to combat all forms of discrimination in the workplace, including sexual and other harassment, as well as forced and child labour. By helping to ensure that safety and health standards are maintained in workplaces, it also contributes to preventing serious occupational accidents and the spread of occupational diseases and HIV/AIDS. Labour inspection is carried out by regular inspections of workplaces in industry, commerce and agriculture, and in many countries in non-commercial services by providing advice and information to employers and workers aimed at better compliance with legal obligations. This service should cooperate with employers' and workers' organizations and should be composed of sufficient qualified staff, including an adequate proportion of women.

The labour inspection service should play an important role in preventing and eliminating discriminatory practices in the workplace. Specifically, it should be ensured that:

*   labour inspectors are given access to the workplace and are freely able to maintain communication with management, as well as with employees of both sexes, if necessary also in the absence of management representatives;

*   labour inspectors address workers' education programmes and training courses on all aspects of their duties, and particularly those that involve the elimination of discrimination and the promotion of equal employment opportunities;

- workers are encouraged to contact the labour inspection service for information and explanations on labour law when problems arise concerning discriminatory practices in employment;

- labour inspectors are informed and trained on all aspects of policies and procedures concerning equal employment opportunities and non-discriminatory treatment, including sexual harassment;

- labour inspectors are recruited from both sexes, are aware of the importance of promoting equality, and understand how this relates to their work; if necessary, women inspectors should be in charge of special women's issues;

- records of discriminatory practices in the workplace and measures or notices of redress are included in labour inspection reports;

- labour inspection reports include labour force data disaggregated by sex.

    C. 81 and R. 81: Labour Inspection, 1947, and Protocol, 1995
    C. 129 and R. 133: Labour Inspection (Agriculture), 1969

➡ See also **Labour administration; Public employment services and private employment agencies**

Labour market

Strictly speaking, the labour market is the context in which the labour force is constituted – the sea in which the labour force swims, so to speak. The labour market is the arena in which jobs and workers are matched, or where labour is exchanged for wages or payment in kind, whereas the labour force comprises the supply of workers to that market. However, the labour force is necessarily shaped by trends in the labour market (such as globalization, informalization of labour etc.).

The labour market and its institutions are not neutral, but reflect power relations in the economy and society at large. Changes in the labour market are therefore gendered and produce changes in the gender structure of the labour force, for instance in occupational segregation, men's and women's relative participation in employment, and so on.

➡ See also **Labour force; Occupational segregation**

Labour statistics

Labour statistics are an essential basis for measuring the extent of discrimination and evaluating equality of opportunity and treatment in employment in both developed and developing countries. The compilation of labour statistics by member States, their publication by the competent national body and their submission to the ILO is required under the provisions of the Labour Statistics Convention, 1985 (No. 160). Labour statistics ought to be carried out to measure, as a minimum:

- the size of the economically active population and the extent of employment, unemployment and underemployment, at least once a year;

- average earnings and hours of work, at least once a year;

- the structure and distribution of the economically active population, including disaggregation by nature of employment (employer, self-employed, employee, unpaid family worker, member of producers' cooperative), every ten years.

These statistics ought always to be classified according to the sex of workers and, whenever possible, age group and branch of economic activity. The availability of sex-disaggregated data and statistical information enables comparative analysis of how women and men fare in work and society, which in turn helps to detect existing discrimination, especially in the less transparent form of indirect discrimination. For instance, the documentation of disparities in pay levels makes it easier to assess the real size of the gender pay gap and its intersections with other forms of pay inequity.

On the whole, data disaggregated by sex are more readily available than those disaggregated by other categories. It is recognized, nonetheless, that there are serious limitations to the data available on the extent and nature of discrimination in general and in particular on sex discrimination. Sometimes this is due to a simple lack of data, sometimes to the fact that the format or structure of readily available data such as censuses and household surveys might not yield information that allows a direct link with discrimination to be made.

The quality of labour statistics is affected by the extent to which they reflect the differences and similarities between men and women in the labour market. Women are an important population in "atypical" work situations, so the production of valid and reliable labour statistics will depend on a clear understanding of the variety of work women perform and how they behave in the labour market. For instance, statistical information on the informal economy is essential if an accurate picture of the contribution of women workers is to be fairly assessed. However, women's contribution to national economies is often under-reported or misreported, and the statistics available are often partial and skewed because of persistent unquestioned assumptions about gender roles in the economy.

    C. 160 and R. 170: Labour Statistics, 1985

→   See also **Labour administration; Labour market**

Lifelong learning

→   See **Education; Employability; Paid educational leave; Social security; Structural unemployment; Vocational guidance; Vocational training; Work–life balance**

M

Marital status

Marital status describes the population according to their civil status as single, married, widowed or divorced. It should not have any influence on any aspect of the work situation of an individual of either sex.

Employment decisions should not be taken on the basis of an individual's marital status. Applicants should not be required to disclose their marital status as part of a pre-employment interview or other selection procedure. A pre-employment inquiry regarding the employment of other family members in the workplace may exceptionally be justified in the interests of preventing nepotism.

Job responsibilities such as travel, entertainment or other duties outside working hours should not be used as a justification for discriminating on the basis of marital status. Full employment benefits should be provided to all workers regardless of their marital status.

> *C. 111 and R. 111: Discrimination (Employment and Occupation), 1958*
> *C. 156 and R. 165: Workers with Family Responsibilities, 1981*
> *C. 158 and R. 166: Termination of Employment, 1982*

➜ See also **Access to employment; Discrimination; Dismissal; Diversity; Family responsibilities, workers with; Selection procedures; Work–family balance**

Maritime labour

The ILO's Maritime Labour Convention, 2006 provides comprehensive rights and protection at work for more than 1.2 million men and women working on ships worldwide. It consolidates and updates 66 international labour standards related to seafarers adopted over the last 80 years. The Convention sets out seafarers' rights to decent work under a wide range of headings, and aims to be globally applicable, easily understandable, readily updatable and uniformly enforced.

Although maritime work has traditionally been a predominantly masculine occupation, women are increasingly engaged in it, and the MLC provides an opportunity for the historically male-biased assumptions of many of the previous standards related to seafarers to be updated and extended effectively to workers of both sexes.

The MLC contains standard provisions on non-discrimination (Art. III, which makes respect for the fundamental conventions mandatory) and on equal pay for work of equal value. It also states, in the context of recruitment and place-ment of seafarers, that the collection of data on age or sex "should be admis-sible only for statistical purposes or if used in the framework of a programme to prevent discrimination based on age or sex" (Guideline B1.4.1 – Organizational and operational guidelines, para. 1 (e)). Otherwise, the equality of provisions covering safety, security, health protection and other conditions of work is implicit and rests on the mandatory compliance with the fundamental conventions against discrimination.

> MLC: Maritime Labour, 2006
> P. 147 Protocol of 1996 to the Merchant Shipping (Minimum Standards) Convention, 1976

Masculinities

The term "masculinities" refers to patterns of conduct linked to men's place in a given set of gender roles and relations. The plural is used because patterns of masculinity vary over time, place and culture. Research based on a gender ana-lysis of men and masculinities which recognizes that unequal gender power rela-tions can also oppress men and boys is a growing field of study to which the ILO has made some specific contributions, notably as regards HIV/AIDS.[18]

➜   See also **Division of labour; Gender analysis; HIV/AIDS**

Maternity leave

Maternity leave is the leave from work to which a woman is entitled for a con-tinuous period before and after giving birth. Convention No. 183 (2000) on maternity protection extends the provisions of Convention No. 103 (1952) by providing that all employed women, including those in atypical forms of depen-dent work, shall be entitled to a period of maternity leave of not less than 14 weeks (Art. 4.1), at least six of which must be taken after the child is born unless otherwise agreed at the national level by the government and the repre-sentative organizations of employers and workers (Art. 4.4). The prenatal

---

[18] See http://www.ilo.org/dyn/gender/genderresources.listhome, search under "Men and masculinities".

portion of maternity leave shall be extended by any period elapsing between the presumed date of childbirth and the actual date of childbirth, without reduction in any compulsory portion of postnatal leave (Art. 4.5).

In the case of illness, complications or risk of complications arising out of pregnancy or childbirth, leave shall be provided before or after the maternity leave period, on production of a medical certificate. The nature and the maximum duration of such leave may be specified in accordance with national law and practice (Art. 5).

Recommendation No. 191 recommends that member States should endeavour to extend the period of maternity leave to at least 18 weeks (Para. 1 (1)), and also that provision should be made for an extension of the maternity leave in the event of multiple births. In practice, collective bargaining agreements between unions and employers can extend the leave entitlement. Many countries have extended the protection against dismissal to a certain period following the employee's return to work after maternity leave.

An essential part of maternity leave is the right to return to the same work, or one with the same pay, upon return from the leave. Convention No. 183 (Art. 8) provides that while a woman is absent from work on maternity leave or during a nationally specified period following her return to work, it shall be unlawful to dismiss her, except on grounds unrelated to the pregnancy or birth of the child and its consequences or nursing and with the burden of proof resting on the employer.

Most countries provide cash benefits to replace partially the income lost during maternity leave. They are part of the larger maternity protection "package" (see *Maternity protection*, p. 128). Without these benefits, many women could not afford to take maternity leave or might be forced to return to work before their health allowed.

In order to promote gender equality and to adapt to the needs of working families, the European Union and many individual countries have adopted legislation in which leave beyond childbirth is granted to either parent.

> *C. 103: Maternity Protection (Revised) and R95: Maternity Protection, 1952*
> *C. 183 and R. 191: Maternity Protection, 2000*
> *C. 110: Plantations, 1958 (and Protocol, 1982)*
> *C. 171: Night Work, 1990*
> *P. 89: Protocol of 1990 to the Night Work (Women) Convention (Revised), 1948*
> *C. 149 and R. 157: Nursing Personnel, 1977*
> *C. 158: Termination of Employment, 1982*
> *R. 165: Workers with Family Responsibilities, 1981*

➔ See also **Cash and medical benefits for maternity; Dismissal; Family responsibilities, workers with; Flexibility of labour; Maternity protection; Nursing personnel; Parental leave; Teachers**

Maternity protection

Maternity protection for employed women is an essential element in equality of opportunity. It seeks to enable women to combine their reproductive and productive roles successfully, and to prevent unequal treatment in employment due to women's reproductive role.

The elements of maternity protection covered by the most recent standards concerned with maternity protection, Convention No. 183 and Recommendation No. 191 (2000), are:

- maternity leave – the mother's right to a period of rest in relation to childbirth (see preceding entry);

- cash and medical benefits – the right to cash benefits during absence for maternity (see p. 31);

- protection of the health of mother and child during pregnancy, childbirth and breastfeeding (see p. 100);

- the mother's right to breastfeed a child after her return to work (see p. 24);

- employment protection and non-discrimination – guaranteeing the woman employment security and the right to return to the same job or an equivalent one with the same pay (see p. 53).

Historically, maternity protection has always been a central concern of the ILO. Among the first international labour standards to be adopted in 1919 was Convention No. 3 concerning the employment of women before and after childbirth. This Convention laid out the basic principles of maternity protection: the right to maternity leave, the right to medical benefits, and the right to income replacement during leave. The right to leave was reinforced by the explicit prohibition of dismissal during a woman's absence on maternity leave or at such time that the notice would expire during such absence. Employment security was thus seen as a vital aspect of maternity protection from the start.

The Maternity Protection Convention (No. 103), of 1952, retained the same principal elements of protection, but the means and manner of providing these benefits were made more explicit:

- The 12-week minimum leave period was to include a period of mandatory post-natal leave of at least six weeks; additional leave was to be provided before or after confinement in the event of medically certified illness arising out of pregnancy or confinement.

- Medical benefits were to include pre-natal, confinement and post-natal care by qualified midwives or medical practitioners, as well as hospitalization if necessary; freedom of choice of doctor and of public or private hospital were to be respected.

- As regards cash benefits, a minimum income replacement rate of two-thirds of the woman's previous earnings was specified for those benefits derived from social insurance; payroll taxes were to be paid on the basis of the total number of workers employed without distinction of sex.

While many of the key elements of Convention 103 are retained in the newest maternity protection standards, Convention No. 183 and Recommendation No. 191, important strengthening provisions include:

- the extension of coverage to all employed women, including those in atypical forms of dependent work (Art. 2.1);

- the extension of the minimum leave period to 14 weeks (Art. 4.1);

- stronger protection from dismissal during pregnancy or maternity leave and after return to work, and the guaranteed right to return to the same position or an equivalent position paid at the same rate at the end of maternity leave (Art. 8);

- the requirement for members to adopt appropriate measures to ensure that maternity does not constitute a source of discrimination in employment, including prohibiting pregnancy tests as part of job candidate selection procedures except in very limited specific circumstances (Art. 9).

Although Convention No. 183 and Recommendation No. 191 are the most up to date standards on maternity protection, the earlier standards remain in force in a number of countries and some countries have ratified one or more of the Conventions but not all three. Convention No. 183 has been ratified by 13 countries, Convention No. 103 by 40, and Convention No. 3 by 33; a total of 61 countries have ratified one or more of the three Conventions.

National laws designed to protect the health of mother and child and the employment rights of working women figure prominently in the legislation of almost every ILO member State. There are, however, significant variations in the scope of coverage, the extent of protection, the complexity of the schemes in force, and the respective responsibilities of the State and of individual employers for the provision of cash benefits.

Typically, a simple package includes the provision, under labour legislation, of leave before and after the birth, often with the payment of cash benefits, whether by the employer, out of social security schemes, through public funds or by a combination of these means. It is declared unlawful for employers to give notice of dismissal during maternity leave and its eventual extension, or at such time as the notice would expire during such leave. Nursing mothers are authorized to take breaks, which are often paid, for breastfeeding.

More comprehensive packages improve on the above provisions in terms of the length of maternity leave, the level of benefits and the length of the period during which employment is protected. They often include a series of measures aimed at protecting the health of the woman and the unborn child, such as the prohibition or limitation of night work or overtime work, and a right to transfer from work that may be detrimental to the outcome of pregnancy either because it is intrinsically dangerous or because it is inadvisable in view of an individual woman's state of health. The health protection measures envisaged for pregnant women often apply also to nursing mothers.

Explicit protection against discrimination on the grounds of pregnancy or motherhood is a feature of the most advanced schemes, for instance that in the European Union. In a growing number of countries, there is also a move towards adopting a parental approach. Under parental schemes, a period of maternity leave is reserved for the mother within a longer period of leave which is available to either or both parents.

In June 2004, the International Labour Conference adopted a Resolution on Gender Equality, Pay Equity and Maternity Protection, which links maternity protection to non-discrimination by calling on all governments to ratify and apply Conventions Nos. 100 and calling on all the social partners to contribute actively to the elimination of gender discrimination and the promotion of gender equality.

> *C. 103: Maternity Protection (Revised) and R. 95: Maternity Protection, 1952*
>
> *C. 183 and R. 191: Maternity Protection, 2000*
>
> *C. 171: Night Work, 1990*
>
> *C. 102: Social Security (Minimum Standards), 1952*
>
> *R. 114: Radiation Protection, 1960*
>
> *R. 116: Reduction of Hours of Work, 1962*
>
> *C. 110: Plantations, 1958 (and Protocol, 1982)*
>
> *R. 157: Nursing Personnel, 1977*
>
> *C. 175: Part-Time Work, 1994*
>
> *C. 177 and R. 184: Home Work, 1996*
>
> *C. 181: Private Employment Agencies, 1997*

→ See also **Atypical work; Biological risks; Breastfeeding workers; Cash and medical benefits for maternity; Health during maternity; Maternity leave; Night work; Part-time work; Public employment services and private employment agencies; Selection procedures; Social security; Teachers**

Migrant workers

Migrant workers are persons who migrate from one country to another with a view to being employed otherwise than on their own account. ILO instruments on migrant workers do not apply to the following: frontier workers; short-term entry of members of the liberal professions and the performing arts; seafarers; persons coming to a country specifically for training or education purposes; and employees of organizations or enterprises operating within the territory of a country who have been admitted temporarily to that country at the request of their employer to undertake specific duties or assignments for a limited and defined period and who are required to leave the country on completion of their duties or assignments.

All migrant workers, irrespective of sex or other personal attributes, should have the right to treatment no less favourable than that applied to national workers in respect of, among other things:

- remuneration (including family allowances);

- hours of work;

- overtime arrangements;

- holidays with pay;

- restrictions on home work;

- minimum age for employment;

- apprenticeship and training;

- women's work and the work of young persons;

- trade union activities;

- participation in and enjoyment of the benefits of collective bargaining;

- accommodation and social security.

Because of high and persistent unemployment, many countries have introduced policies to reduce the number of immigrants and are now confronted with the problem of migrant workers who are in an irregular situation and/or illegally employed. Although the statistical evidence is not clear, it can be assumed that a great many of these workers are women. Gender-blind immigration policies in destination countries can have disproportionately negative effects on women immigrants and leave them at higher risk of irregular employment and deportation.

Women migrant workers tend to be employed in a restricted range of occupations, including manual work in agriculture, factories or EPZs, but mostly jobs related to stereotypical female roles as caregivers, nurses, domestic workers, and low-status workers in the catering, hotel, and entertainment industries. By the very nature of the work they undertake, women and girls can be particularly vulnerable when employed for work outside their own countries. They may be subject to exploitation and abuse not only because they are outside the legal protection of their country of origin, but also because they often hold jobs for which there is little protection under social legislation Their situation is often made worse by the lack of autonomy and the strong relationship of subordination that are typical of these jobs. They may be subject to gender-based violence and sexual abuse, especially if they are working as domestics or sex workers. In addition, these women are usually young, poor, and isolated from their families, whom they have left in their countries of origin. They do not speak the language of the host country, are unaware that they have rights that are being infringed, and usually do not know where to go for help. At worst, they may be victims of coercive recruitment and employment practices or human trafficking. Young women and girls are at particular risk of being trafficked for commercial sexual exploitation.

Most ILO protective provisions concerning migrant workers apply to immigrants who have been regularly admitted to the territory of a member State. Convention No. 97, for instance, calls on States to apply treatment without discrimination in respect of sex to immigrants lawfully within its territory. The Migrant Workers (Supplementary Provisions) Convention, 1975 (No. 143) was the first attempt by the international community to deal with the problems arising from clandestine migration and the illegal employment of migrants. That instrument, inter alia:

- lays down the general obligation to respect the basic human rights of all migrant workers, whether or not they entered the country on a regular basis;

- calls on member States to guarantee equality of treatment, with regard to working conditions, for all migrant workers who perform the same activity whatever might be the particular conditions of their employment (Art. 12 (g));

- guarantees a number of rights arising out of past employment (as regards remuneration, social security and other benefits) to ensure that illegally employed migrant workers are not deprived of their rights in respect of the work actually performed;

- grants the right of appeal to the migrant worker;

- calls on member States to suppress clandestine movements of migrants for employment and illegal employment, and to sanction the organizers of illicit or clandestine movements of migrants for employment and those who employ workers who have immigrated in illegal conditions.

This Convention does not lay down any specific obligation with regard to combating the exploitation of women migrant workers. However, female irregular migrant workers, including the victims of trafficking, are effectively protected under Convention No. 29 on forced labour.

> *C. 29: Forced Labour, 1930*
> *C. 97 and R. 86: Migration for Employment (Revised), 1949*
> *C. 143: Migrant Workers (Supplementary Provisions), 1975 and*
> *R. 151: Migrant Workers, 1975*
> *Declaration on Fundamental Principles and Rights at Work, 1998*

➜   See also **Clandestine work; Forced labour; Trafficking in persons**

Millennium Development Goals

The Millennium Development Goals (MDGs) are based on UN Millennium Declaration, signed in September 2000 at the UN Millennium Summit. They set out an ambitious agenda for halving poverty and achieving other development targets by 2015.

The eight MDGs are:

1. Eradicate extreme poverty and hunger.

2. Achieve universal primary education.

3. Promote gender equality and empower women.

4. Reduce child mortality.

5. Improve maternal health.

6. Combat HIV/AIDS, malaria and other diseases.

7. Ensure environmental sustainability.

8. Develop a global partnership for development.

For the ILO, the MDGs are firmly linked with the Decent Work Agenda, which contributes to meeting all eight MDGs through decent and productive employment, social protection, rights at work and social dialogue.[19] Based on the conviction that decent, productive jobs are the most effective route out of

---

[19] For detailed information see ILO, *External Relations and Partnerships, Information folder on Decent Work and the Millennium Development Goals.* Available at: http://www.ilo.org/bureau/exrel/mdg/briefs/.

poverty, the ILO considers that the MDGs and the Decent Work Agenda go hand in hand and reinforce each other as instruments for promoting equality between men and women. At the same time, promoting gender equality and eliminating gender-based discrimination are essential to eradicating poverty.

Gender equality is highly relevant to the achievement of all the MDGs, but the third goal refers specifically to gender equality. MDG 3 uses women's share in non-agricultural waged employment (together with the ratio of girls to boys in education, the ratio of literate females to males aged 15–24, and the proportion of seats in national parliaments held by women) as an indicator for gender equality and women's empowerment, reflecting the importance the UN attaches to women's access to employment. Within the UN system, the ILO takes the lead in reporting on trends concerning the rate of women's non-agricultural wage employment and also on the unemployment rate among young people aged 15–24.

➜   See also **Decent work; Education; Gender equality; Youth employ-ment**

Mines

Mines are defined as surface or underground sites where the exploration and preparation for and the extraction of minerals takes place.

The Underground Work (Women) Convention, 1935 (No. 45) provided that, in principle, no female of any age should be employed in underground work in mines. Reflecting the shift of emphasis in standard setting from specific protection for women workers to equal protection for all workers, a new instrument concerning safety and health in mines, Convention No. 176, was adopted in 1995. Focusing on the protection of all employees, male or female, in mines, this Convention covers a wide range of measures to be implemented by the competent authorities and the social partners concerning:

•   the supervision and inspection of safety and health in mines;

•   the procedures for reporting and investigating fatal and serious accidents, dangerous occurrences and mine disasters;

•   the compilation and publication of statistics on accidents, occupational diseases and dangerous occurrences;

•   the power of the competent authority to suspend or restrict mining activities on safety and health grounds;

- the establishment of effective procedures to ensure the implementation of the rights of workers and their representatives to be adequately trained, informed and consulted on matters relating to safety and health at the workplace.

Employers should take all necessary measures to eliminate or minimize the risks to safety in mines under their control. This implies the preparation of emergency plans, training, information and protection of workers.

Under Convention No. 176, workers are granted the right to report accidents, dangerous occurrences and hazards, to request and obtain inspections and investigations, to be informed of workplace hazards, to leave the worksite in dangerous situations, and to collectively select safety and health representatives. Workers also have the duty to comply with the prescribed measures, to take reasonable care of their own safety and health and that of other persons, to report risks and to cooperate with the employer to permit compliance with his or her duties.

Only a small number of women work in large mines, but the number in small-scale mining reaches almost one-third of the workforce. Overall, the proportion of women workers in mines ranges from less than 10 per cent (in Asia) up to 60 per cent (in some mining areas in Africa). Many of them work part-time, and under particularly harsh conditions with poor remuneration.

C. 176 and R. 183: Safety and Health in Mines, 1995

➜ See **Labour inspection; Occupational safety and health; Part-time work**

Minimum wage

The primary goal of the adoption of a minimum wage policy is to set a floor for a national wage structure so as to protect low-waged earners. It is designed to improve the earnings of those disproportionately represented at the bottom end of the occupational hierarchy, namely women, migrants, and other groups susceptible to discrimination. There is evidence that in some countries women have benefited from a minimum wage policy, although equalizing wages can often mean lowering the wage levels of both men and women rather than raising them, and this tendency should be guarded against. In contexts where trade unions are not well represented (and where women are under-represented in trade unions), a minimum wage may be a useful component of an approach towards achieving pay equity between men and women.

However, in some countries, for example in Eastern Europe, a tendency towards differentiating the minimum wage applicable to different categories of worker is emerging, with clear implications for the widening of a gender pay gap.

A minimum wage policy is often considered irrelevant to self-employed workers, most of whom are women, especially in developing countries. However,
there is some evidence to suggest that the existence of a minimum wage may
provide a benchmark or reference point for earnings and may thus become a
useful bargaining chip for workers in the informal economy.

> *R. 30: Minimum Wage-Fixing Machinery, 1928*
> *R. 89: Minimum Wage-Fixing Machinery (Agriculture), 1951*
> *R. 90: Equal Remuneration, 1951*
> *C. 131 and R. 135: Minimum Wage Fixing, 1970*

➜ See also **Collective bargaining; Equal remuneration**

Mobbing

➜ See **Harassment and pressure**

| N

Night work

The development of ILO standards dealing with night work offers a clear demonstration of the shift from the original concept of protecting women against excessively arduous working conditions towards an understanding that protection appropriate to the nature of the work should in principle be granted to all workers irrespective of sex, reflecting the present-day principles of non-discrimination at work and gender equity. There is growing support for the view that, with the exception of standards and benefits related to maternity protection, all other special protective measures do not serve the objectives of equal opportunities and equal treatment of men and women. If some women do not tolerate night work as well as men, that is not a result of biological differences but of women's exhausting double burden of housework and waged work, to which a more strategic and gender-equitable response is to promote the redistribution of domestic labour, for example via Convention No. 156 on Workers with Family Responsibilities.

Accordingly, the revised Night Work (Women) Convention, 1948 (No. 89) has been effectively replaced by the Night Work Convention, 1990 (No. 171) and its accompanying Recommendation No. 178. A Protocol enlarging the flexibility of Convention No. 89 was also adopted in 1990.

According to Convention No. 171, all workers, regardless of sex, working during the night should be protected by specific measures, including:

* health protection (first-aid facilities, health checks);

* maternity protection;

* social services;

* opportunities for occupational advancement;

* additional compensation (hours of work, pay or similar benefits).

Exempt from the scope of this Convention are workers employed in the agriculture, stock-raising, fishing, maritime, transport and inland navigation sectors who work during the night. The "night" is now defined as at least seven consecutive hours which include the hours between midnight and 5 a.m. In agricultural enterprises, the employment of women during the night should be regulated so as to ensure that they have a period of rest consisting of no less than nine hours, which ought to be consecutive.

A female night worker should be transferred to day work or have her maternity leave extended before and after childbirth for a period of at least 16 weeks, of which at least eight should be before the expected date of childbirth. During this period, the woman:

* should not be dismissed or given notice of dismissal except for justifiable reasons not connected with pregnancy or childbirth;

* should be guaranteed an income at a level sufficient for the upkeep of herself and her child; and

* should not lose the benefits regarding status, seniority and access to promotion which may be attached to her regular night work position.

Shift work has potential negative effects on workers' health and safety, especially where it is carried out at night. While several of the effects are not gender-specific, a specific health risk for women entailed by shift work carried out at night is an increased risk of breast cancer (ILO, 2004e and ILO, 2004g).

C. 171 and R. 178: Night Work, 1990
P. 89: Protocol of 1990 to the Night Work (Women) Convention (Revised), 1948
C. 156 and R. 165: Workers with Family Responsibilities, 1981

➔ See also **Dismissal; Gender equity; Maternity leave; Family responsibilities, workers with; Work–family balance**

Non-standard work

➔ See **Atypical work**

Non-traditional occupations

Although women's presence in occupations that are not "traditionally" regarded as suitable for them, particularly in the scientific and technical fields, is growing, it is still far from equal to that of men. Worldwide, women's employment is concentrated in a relatively small number of branches of economic activity (see *Occupational segregation*, p. 144). This restricted presence contributes to creating stereotypes of women and excludes them from professions that are better remunerated.

On the other hand, boys and men also tend to be corralled into occupations traditionally thought of as masculine – construction, engineering, finance, the military, and so on. They should also have equal access to the traditionally feminized professions, such as teaching, nursing and care work.

Horizontal occupational segregation by sex has its roots at least in part in gender inequalities in education and vocational training systems. Each member State should therefore review its employment and education policies so as to:

- ensure that technical subjects are available and are offered on an equal; basis to all students at primary and secondary levels;

- strive for better gender balance in teaching staff in all disciplines;

- facilitate equal access for women and men to polytechnic and vocational training institutions;

- promote female students in non-traditional subjects for women and male students in non-traditional subjects for men, at university level;

- promote the greater employment of women in the scientific and technical sector.

In some cases special affirmative measures may be necessary for one sex or the other.

> C. 168: Employment Promotion and Protection against Unemployment, 1988
> R. 169: Employment Policy (Supplementary Provisions), 1984
> C. 142 and R. 150: Human Resources Development, 1975
> R. 195: Human Resources Development, 2004

→ See also **Affirmative action; Education; Human resources development; Nursing personnel; Occupational segregation; Teachers; Youth employment**

Nursing personnel

Nursing personnel are all categories of persons providing nursing care and nursing services for remuneration. The requirements for the practice of nursing should be specified by national legislation, and the practice of nursing should be limited to persons who meet these requirements.

All nursing personnel, irrespective of sex or other attributes, should enjoy conditions at least equivalent to those of other workers as regards working hours (including overtime), weekly rest, paid annual leave, educational leave, maternity leave, sick leave and social security, and equal pay for work of equal value.

Nursing personnel should undergo medical examinations on taking up and terminating an appointment and at regular intervals during their services. However, pregnancy, if detected by such an examination, should not form grounds for the dismissal of the worker. While HIV-positive status is an unacceptable ground of discrimination, nursing is one of the occupations in which a person's HIV-positive status should be taken into account when his or her fitness for a job is being assessed; however, in these cases, the burden of proof of unfitness for the job should rest on the employer.

Nursing personnel should not be exposed to special risks. Where this is unavoidable, measures should be taken to minimize exposure to these risks. Nurses who are pregnant or parents of young children and whose normal assignment could be prejudicial to their health or that of their child should be transferred, without loss of entitlements, to work appropriate to the circumstances.

Studies should be undertaken and kept up to date to determine special occupational risks to which nursing personnel may be exposed so that these risks may be prevented. Appropriate measures should be taken for supervising the application of provisions concerning the protection of the health and safety of nursing personnel. In particular, the collaboration of nursing personnel and their organizations should be sought in ensuring the effective application of such provisions.

Nursing is a profession which remains female-dominated. Men should be given equal opportunities in the profession and encouraged to make nursing a career.

C. 149: Nursing Personnel, 1977 and R. 157: Nursing Personnel, 1977

➜ See also **Care work; Hours of work; Maternity protection; Night work; Paid educational leave; Social protection; Social security**

O

Occupational health services

→ See **Occupational safety and health**; see also **Labour administration; Labour inspection**

Occupational safety and health

Occupational safety and health (OSH) – the prevention and reduction of occupational and work-related accidents, injuries, and diseases through the improvement of working conditions and work environments – has been a key concern of the ILO since its foundation.

The long-term objectives of the ILO's activities in the field of OSH are:

* reducing the number and seriousness of occupational accident and diseases;

* adapting the working environment, working conditions, equipment and work processes to the physical and mental capacities of all workers;

* enhancing the physical, mental and social well-being of male and female workers in all occupations;

* encouraging national policies on OSH and preventive action programmes, and supplying ILO constituents with appropriate assistance to facilitate their implementation.

As women's participation in the labour force has increased, the gender-specific aspects of occupational accidents and diseases have been recognized. Agriculture, for example, remains a high-risk sector for both women and men, but many women working in agriculture end up doing the worst jobs, such as working with pesticides, chemical or biological agents without protection, or doing heavy cultivation or harvesting work without mechanical assistance.

Segregation by occupation leads to exposure to health risks and hazards peculiar to those occupations, which affects the over-represented sex more than the other. In industry, women factory workers in export-processing zones (where they are the majority) endure long hours at non-ergonomic work stations and often work with unprotected machinery. Industrial machinery is generally designed for men and is often awkward and tiring for women (and small men) to operate. In microelectronics, another industry where women predominate, they are exposed to chemicals which can have carcinogenic effects. On the other hand, work in sectors where men predominate, such as construction or the oil industry, generates its own set of hazards and health risks.

Over the years, the focus of gender issues in OSH has shifted from the protection of women based on an assumed difference between all women and all men to the equalization of rights and protection for all workers, male and female, and the idea of making the workplace safe for each individual worker, whatever their sex or other personal attributes. Legislation oriented towards the protection of women as mothers and wives (which was assumed to be their primary function) was revealed to have potentially discriminatory effects on women's job opportunities. The focus is now on removing the risk from the workplace in the interests of protecting the health of all workers rather than excluding any social group from hazardous occupations. This new orientation has led to the revision or replacement of a number of OSH-related standards, for example those related to night work (see p. 138)

Work-related stress is increasingly being recognized as an OSH issue. Both men and women suffer from stress, but for different reasons, which may require different healthcare responses. Women's multiple roles at work and in the family means that they tend to suffer additionally from stress and fatigue.

Following on from a reference in the Resolution on equal opportunities and treatment adopted by the International Labour Conference in 1985 to the need to protect men and women from risks inherent in their work, the Conclusions of the 2003 Conference made explicit the connection between safe work and decent work and raised "the need to take account of gender-specific factors in the context of OSH standards, other instruments, management systems and practice".

The following are some ways in which gender equality can be addressed in OSH:

- Health promotion policies should be based on more accurate information about the relationship between OSH and gender issues.

- Epidemiological research into the effects of hazards on occupationally defined populations should be critically assessed for bias so as to avoid assumptions based on gender stereotypes.

- Occupational health services, whose function is preventive, should include analysis of the different health situations and needs of male and female workers in their study of work methods, conditions of work and factors in the working environment that may cause diseases or injuries.

- Health promotion policies for working women and men should take into account their different roles in the workplace, home and community, examining the health effects of each role and their possible interaction or accumulation.

- A broad strategy for the improvement of women workers' safety and health must be included in national OSH policies, especially in fields where there is a high concentration of women.

- Specific preventive programmes should be implemented at the organization or enterprise level.

- When providing counselling to employers on OSH issues, occupational health services should highlight relevant gender issues and propose gender-sensitive responses.

- Ergonomic considerations (maximum weight, national standards for manual handling, etc.) should be directed away from setting different limits for male and female workers to a system based on individual human variability irrespective of sex, age or ethnic characteristics.

- Broad generalizations about women's (and men's) physical capacities should be avoided, and standards at national level should be adopted to provide adequate protection from any hazard for the most susceptible or vulnerable workers irrespective of sex or other attributes.

- Special legal protection for women workers should not be invalidated but should be extended to male workers where appropriate, e.g. in the case of radiation protection and reproductive health.

- Women should be more equally represented in all decision-making processes concerning the protection of their health.

- Equal protection from workplace hazards for all workers should be accompanied by encouraging more equal sharing of the workload between women and men in both the workplace and the domestic sphere.

C. 102: Social Security (Minimum Standards), 1952
C. 110: Plantations, 1958
C. 115 and R114: Radiation Protection, 1960
C. 118: Equality of Treatment (Social Security),
C. 139 and R. 147: Occupational Cancer, 1974
C. 148 and R. 156: Working Environment (Air Pollution,
Noise and Vibration), 1977
C. 149 and R. 157: Nursing Personnel, 1977
C. 155 and R. 164: Occupational Safety and Health, 1981
C. 156 and R. 165: Workers with Family Responsibilities, 1981
Protocol of 2002 to the Occupational Safety and Health Convention, 1981 (No. 155)

C. 161 and R. 171: Occupational Health Services, 1985
C. 162 and R. 172: Asbestos, 1986
C. 167 and R. 175: Construction, 1988
C. 170 and R. 177: Chemicals, 1990
C. 171 and R. 178: Night Work, 1990
Protocol of 1990 to the Night Work (Women) Convention (Revised), 1948 (No. 89)
C. 174 and R. 181: Prevention of Major Industrial Accidents, 1993
C. 183 and R. 191: Maternity Protection, 2000
C. 184 and R. 192: Safety and Health in Agriculture, 2001
C. 187 and R. 197: Promotional Framework for Occupational Safety
        and Health, 2006
R. 97: Protection of Workers' Health, 1953
R. 102: Welfare Facilities, 1956
R. 116: Reduction of Hours of Work, 1962
R. 194: List of Occupational Diseases, 2002

➜ See also **Agricultural and other rural workers; Chemicals; Hygiene in the workplace; Maternity protection; Radiation protection; Social protection**

Occupational segregation

Occupational segregation by sex occurs when women and men are concentrated in different types and at different levels of activity and employment. Worldwide, labour markets are segregated to a surprisingly large extent: some 60% of non-agricultural workers in the world are in an occupation where at least 80% of the workers are either women or men. Women tend to be confined to a different range of occupations than men are (horizontal segregation) and to lower job grades (vertical segregation). In the 1980s and 1990s, the range of occupations in which women were employed expanded in many countries – especially some OECD countries and some small developing countries where occupational segregation was high – but narrowed in others, particularly in transitional economies. It seems, however, that as horizontal segregation fades, vertical segregation often intensifies (ILO, 2003, p. xi) even when new occupations open up to women, such as computer programming and other ICT-related work, gender imbalances within them persist.

This situation rarely stems from direct discrimination through legislation that limits women's access to training and employment. In some countries, however, legislation sets limitations on the kind of work women can do, and this has generally been based on the idea that women's reproductive function must not be put at risk – an idea that is by now on the whole outdated with a few exceptions. Under the Resolution of 1985 on equal opportunities and equal treatment for men and women in employment, when women are excluded from occupation by legislation, there is a need for periodic review to see whether the situation has changed.

The causes of occupational segregation are usually to be found in practices based on entrenched stereotypes and prejudices concerning the roles of women and men in society, including indirect discrimination in education systems. Occupational segregation is an expression of inequality, as it implies differentials in power, skills, income and opportunities.

Even though women are now fast entering the technical occupations and ICT work in greater numbers in some regions of the world, they are still present in fewer occupations than men, and are under-represented at senior management level almost everywhere. They are in the majority in agriculture and services. Women predominate at lower levels in education, health and social services – all occupations related to caring – whereas men predominate in occupations assumed to require physical strength, such as construction and mining, or physical or psychological aggressiveness, such as high finance, politics or the military. In teaching, women are concentrated in pre-primary and primary schools and are under-represented at university level. In health care, women are concentrated in nursing and less represented in the higher professions such as those of physician and surgeon. In commerce and services, women are over-represented among secretaries, salespersons, and catering or cleaning staff, while men are over-represented among drivers and security staff. In management and administration, women usually appear in human resources departments, seldom in finance and strategic management positions.

Differences in the working patterns of women and men may also have a negative impact on the career prospects particularly of women. In countries where flexible working hours and flexible working conditions are common, the large majority of part-time or other non-standard workers are women.

Policies aiming to reduce or eliminate segregation are described as "desegregation policies". Affirmative action policies are of particular importance in correcting occupational segregation. The shares of paid and unpaid work should be distributed more evenly. Measures which help men and women reconcile their work with household and family responsibilities are of particular importance.

C. 111 and R. 111: Discrimination (Employment and Occupation), 1958
C. 142: Human Resources Development, 1975

➜ See also **Affirmative action; Discrimination; Human resources development; Non-traditional occupations; Nursing personnel; Teachers**

Old-age benefit

→   See **Pensions**

Older women workers

The age structure of the world's population is shifting to different degrees according to country or region, but generally upwards. Developing-country populations in general are ageing faster than those of developed countries, but the increase in the population of older women is more marked in developed countries. Older persons worldwide are mostly women; in 2005, they constituted 53 per cent of the over-60 age group and 63 per cent of the over-80 age group (UN, 2007). Labour force participation rates for all workers over 50 have increased worldwide and are likely to continue doing so; but while previously high LFPRs for men, particularly those over 55, are declining, LFPRs for women are increasing.

Older women workers are vulnerable to double or even multiple discrimination on grounds of sex, age and other forms of discrimination such as race/ethnicity. Forms of discrimination that affect women throughout their lives may be compounded as they get older by age-based discrimination. For older women workers any combination of these forms of discrimination can substantially reduce their choices for work or working arrangements, for instance forcing them to shift to part-time or informal work or self-employment. This can, in turn, entail poorer working conditions and inadequate remuneration, making retirement insecure or not a viable choice. Age discrimination against older women workers also means that employers may be neglecting to tap into the skills, experience and commitment of workers who could otherwise contribute productively.

Older women workers also face a form of discrimination not often recognized in law or society that is based on past or continuing family responsibilities. Any assumption that the penalization of women workers because of their family responsibilities would end once they were older is misplaced. Older women workers, especially those who in their younger years spent extended periods outside waged work so as to look after families, must later contend with the view that they may not have updated skills, again limiting their employment opportunities. In addition, older women workers may in fact still have family responsibilities. Whether caring for spouses, elderly relatives, or even grandchildren, older women tend to be more responsible for family care more than older men. For example, the loss of a generation created by HIV/AIDS in many countries in Africa has left grandparents (notably grandmothers) as the chief or sole carers for grandchildren. Work–family balance policies are needed not only by younger women and men workers but by workers of all ages. The ability of older women workers to earn a living for themselves and other disadvantaged family members may in fact hinge on the availability and accessibility of work–family balance policies in the workplace.

Age discrimination in the form of an overt imposition of age limits for hiring or retraining, or indirect discrimination through measures that create conditions that force older workers to retire early, tends to affect women more than men, for instance in mandatory retirement saving schemes. Although actuarial calculations take into account that women tend to live longer than men, one of the main obstacles to their receiving an equivalent retirement pension is that they may not have made continuous payments to such schemes or may not have achieved a minimum number of years of payment over their working life. Interruptions or non-payment into a retirement pension scheme can affect the amount paid back to them later in life. This affects women who stay at home or leave paid employment periodically to raise children or meet other family responsibilities.

The statutory retirement age varies from country to country and even within countries and industries. It may also vary according to sex, the retirement age for women usually being lower than that for men. Women face a much higher risk than men of a drastic drop in living standards when they retire, with lower lifetime earnings and smaller pension entitlements linked to labour market participation. Again, discrimination occurs because the women's work as unpaid carers has traditionally not been acknowledged in retirement pension calculations. A few countries, such as France, have begun to factor this into their calculation of retirement benefits for older women. Still, much more needs to be done in other countries to raise awareness of this problem, to ensure that older women have financial security in retirement and to recognize the importance of work beyond the workplace in retirement pension calculations.

Older Workers Recommendation, 1980 (No. 162) is the ILO's only specific instrument referring to this group, and it does not have the binding force of a Convention. It addresses discrimination on the grounds of age but does not take into account the compounding of this discrimination by other factors, including sex. Neither does the Termination of Employment Recommendation, 1982 (No. 166) take specific account of sex discrimination in its provisions regarding older workers, although the Private Employment Agencies Recommendation, 1997 (No. 188) does include both age and sex as prohibited grounds for discrimination. Convention No. 111 does not list age as one of the seven chief grounds on which discrimination is prohibited in international law, though it does, in Article 1.1 (b), enable member States individually to add emerging grounds of discrimination to the original seven, and some countries have added age to the list. Art. 5.2 of the Convention lists age among the legitimate grounds for special measures designed to meet particular requirements, which are deemed not to be discriminatory.

A lifecycle approach is a useful strategy for addressing compound discrimination on the basis of both sex and age. It is used in the Beijing Platform for Action to capture the prevalence and incidence of discriminatory practices which affect women at different stages of their life. It analyses discrimination in terms of the accumulation of forms of discrimination that can affect a person throughout the different stages of life, and takes into account the positive contribution to society made by workers at different stages – including, for women workers, the stage where a woman's role is principally that of an unpaid carer. A life-cycle approach helps ensure that discrimination encountered by a woman at one stage of life is not perpetuated at later stages (ILO, Gender Promotion Programme, 2001).

> *C. 111 and R. 111: Discrimination (Employment and Occupation), 1958*
> *R. 162: Older workers, 1980*
> *C. 156 and R. 165: Workers with Family Responsibilities, 1981*
> *R. 188: Private Employment Agencies, 1997*
> *R. 189: Job Creation in Small and Medium-Sized Enterprises, 1998*
> *R. 195: Human Resources Development, 2004*

➜ See also **Care work; Diversity in the workplace; Employment relationship; Human resources development; Illness in the family, leave for; Pensions; Work–family balance**

Ombud's offices

➜ See **Remedies and sanctions**

Own-account workers

➜ See **Self-employed workers**

P

Paid educational leave

Paid educational leave is granted to workers for educational purposes for a specified period during working hours, with adequate financial entitlements. Such leave should be granted to all workers on an equal basis without discrimination on the grounds of race, colour, sex, religion, political opinion, national extraction or social origin.

Paid educational leave should be accorded for:

- training at any level;
- general, social and civil education;
- trade union education.

It should allow, without discrimination of any kind:

- the acquisition, improvement and adaptation of occupational and functional skills;
- the competent and active participation of workers and their representatives in the life of the community;
- the human, social and cultural advancement of workers;
- continuing education and training (lifelong learning).

The period of paid educational leave should be considered as a period of effective service for all entitlements.

C140: Paid Educational Leave, 1974

➔ See also **Education; Vocational training**

Parental leave

Parental leave is leave granted to either parent in order to care for a child. It generally follows a period of maternity leave, to which only the mother is entitled. In some countries, parental leave is granted in the event of adoption as well. It may be combined with part-time work arrangements.

Parental leave is different from paternity leave, which is leave for the father at the time of the confinement.

Either parent should have the possibility of obtaining leave of absence for child-care purposes:

- within a period immediately following maternity leave;

- in case of illness of a dependent child;

- for other reasons connected with the upbringing of a child.

In order to promote gender equality, a growing number of countries have passed parental leave legislation in various forms and under various conditions, some of which provide for cash benefits to be paid during the leave period. In the European Union for instance, a new supranational instrument on parental leave was adopted in 1996.

Parental leave, usually unremunerated, is becoming more widespread, though the duration and conditions for taking this leave of absence vary enormously between countries and enterprises. However, mothers rather than fathers tend to be the large majority of those who take up parental leave provisions. A few countries have introduced specific regulations to encourage fathers' take-up of parental leave, for example by reserving a portion of the leave that can be taken only by fathers ("use it or lose it" provisions), providing extensions of paid leave when the father uses some leave and making leaves non-transferable (EC, EU-EGGSIE, 2005, p. 60).

> *C. 156 and R. 165: Workers with Family Responsibilities, 1981*
> *C. 183 and R. 191: Maternity Protection, 2000*

➡ See also **Family responsibilities, workers with; Flexibility of labour; Illness in the family, leave for; Maternity leave; Teachers**

Part-time workers

A part-time worker is an employed person whose normal hours of work are less than those of comparable full-time workers with the same type of employment relationship or similar type of work in the same branch of activity. Transfer from full-time to part-time work or vice versa should be voluntary, as suggested in Recommendation No. 182 (Paras 18–20; see also Recommendation No. 165, Para. 21 (3)). While many countries do not define part-time work, laws or regulations dealing with specific aspects of employment often set certain eligibility requirements or qualifying conditions in the form of minimum earnings or a minimum number of hours worked below which workers are not entitled to certain benefits, in particular social security benefits.

Many temporary workers work part-time, but part-time workers often have longer-term or even permanent contracts. Also, although part-time jobs often have poor employment conditions, a few countries, most notably the Netherlands, have made significant progress towards equal treatment of part-timers. As regards flexibility in hours of work, an important recent development is the acquisition of legal rights for individuals to choose their working hours, occurring first in the Netherlands and Germany.

Measures should be taken at all levels, to ensure that part-time workers receive the same protection as comparable full-time workers in respect of:

- freedom of association and collective bargaining;

- occupational safety and health;

- discrimination.

National policies should also be designed and carried out to ensure that part-time workers receive treatment equivalent to comparable full-time workers with regard to:

- remuneration;

- job security;

- maternity protection;

- statutory social security;

- working conditions, including holidays and sick leave.

One of the most significant features of part-time work is its concentration among women. Many of these women workers earn low wages, lack social protection and benefits, and have few prospects of improving their employment situation. In recent years, a large number of part-time jobs have been created which women are ready to accept more easily than men. Such jobs, however, are often precarious and do not provide for sufficient independent income, and labour law and social security protection. According less favourable opportunities and treatment to part-time workers relative to full-time workers, for instance in wages, company-provided benefits, social protection, career development and in-service vocational training, and access to trade unions, constitutes indirect discrimination against them.

Women do not always accept part-time work as a deliberate choice; they may feel forced to do so because of their double burden of work in employment and in the family, and because full-time work is not available. Parental leave provisions for fathers and mothers, sufficient childcare facilities and more flexible working conditions are therefore desirable options for promoting gender equality in employment for part-time workers. The provisions in Recommendation No. 165 (Para. 21) aimed at regulating the terms and conditions under which part-time and temporary workers and homeworkers are employed and at protecting their employment security stem from the recognition that it is to a large extent workers with family responsibilities who take on part-time and other atypical forms of work. Such terms and conditions should be, as far as possible, equivalent to those of full-time and permanent workers; in appropriate cases, their entitlement may be calculated on a pro-rata basis.

> *R. 165: Workers with Family Responsibilities, 1981*
> *C. 175 and R. 182: Part-Time Work, 1994*
> *R. 191: Maternity Protection, 2000*
> *R. 198: Employment Relationship, 2006*

➜ See also **Atypical work; Casual work; Childcare and family services and facilities; Family responsibilities, workers with; Precarious work; Teachers**

Paternity leave

Paternity leave is a short period of leave taken by a father around the time of the birth of his child. Some countries make specific provisions for this leave. Paternity leave does not yet feature in any international standards, but it is becoming increasingly common in national law and in enterprise practice, and particularly in collective bargaining agreements. The duration of paternity leave ranges between 2 and 15 days, and it is usually paid.

In some countries where there is no specific paternity leave, a more general emergency leave or family leave can be used by new fathers.

> *C. 156 and R. 165: Workers with Family Responsibilities, 1981*
> *C. 183 and R. 191: Maternity Protection, 2000*

➜ See **Family responsibilities, workers with; Parental leave**

Pay equity

➜ See **Equal remuneration**

Pensions

All workers, irrespective of sex or other personal attributes, should be protected by a pension system financed by the contributions of active workers and employers. The pension is a periodical payment that is payable to retired persons after the prescribed age. The prescribed age limit should not be more than 65 years.

The benefit is secured after the person has completed a prescribed period of contributions (normally 30 years of contributions or employment). A reduced benefit may be secured after at least 15 years of contributions or employment. A reduced benefit can also be paid under certain conditions to a person who has not fulfilled the contribution period or the employment conditions required. This benefit may be suspended or reduced if the person undertakes any gainful activity.

In countries where there is the opportunity for women to take earlier retirement, it should be possible for them to choose to remain in work up to the same age as is set for men. In the European Union, for example, the fact that a worker has reached the minimum age for retirement under the pension scheme gives the employer no right to dismiss them.

> *C. 102: Social Security (Minimum Standards), 1952*
> *C. 128: Invalidity, Old Age and Survivors' Benefits, 1967*

➜ See also **Older women workers; Social protection; Social security**

Performance appraisal

Performance appraisal is defined by the ILO as the assessment of employees' performance and capabilities. It is normally carried out by superiors but can also be conducted by one's peers, one's subordinates or oneself. Equity is clearly a key aspect of performance appraisal since systems and procedures need to be seen as fair by all parties.

However, practice shows that the process is open to gender bias and stereotyping. While performance appraisal criteria, such as skill and output and their equivalents, might not be discriminatory per se as a basis for wage differentiation, for instance, there is a danger that insistence on "equal conditions as regards work, skill and output" can be used as a pretext for paying women lower wages than their male counterparts. Unequal access to training and career development opportunities for women, the relative weight given to technical and personal competencies or different perceptions by women and men as to what are the most important factors for career advancement may also result in their faring less well in performance appraisal processes.

Enterprises and organizations need to design and implement performance appraisal systems and procedures with careful attention to criteria that may be gender-inequitable.

> *R. 195: Human Resources Development, 2004*

➜   See also **Human resources development; Vocational training**

Plantation workers

A plantation is a large estate that is planted with cash crops, often for the purpose of export. Women workers form an important component of plantation labour forces, whose rights are covered in the Plantations Convention, 1958 (No. 110).

In accordance with Convention No. 183 of 2000, plantation workers, like other workers, should be entitled to maternity leave. The period of maternity leave must be at least 12 weeks, and not less than six weeks' leave is to be taken after the child is born. It should be possible for the leave period to be extended when childbirth is later than expected or in the case of illness. There may be a qualifying period for maternity leave, which may not exceed a total of 150 days' work with the same employer during the 12 months before childbirth.

No pregnant woman should be required to undertake any type of work which may be harmful to her health. Cash benefits should be provided to ensure the full and healthy maintenance of mother and child. As with other workers, medical benefits should include prenatal, confinement and post-natal care, as well as hospital care where necessary.

A female plantation worker should not be dismissed because she is pregnant, on maternity leave or a nursing mother. She should be entitled to interrupt her work to nurse her child.

> *C. 110: Plantations, 1958 (and Protocol 1982)*
> *R. 110: Plantations, 1958*

➜   See also **Agricultural and other rural workers; Chemicals; Breast-feeding workers; Dismissal; Maternity protection; Maternity leave**

Positive measures

➜   See **Affirmative action**

Precarious work

Precarious work is characterized by a combination of factors:

- a limited duration or a high probability of the worker's losing the job;
- little or no opportunity for workers to control the working conditions;
- absence of benefits or social security provision;
- a low income in tandem with poverty. (Rodgers, 1989)

Worldwide, women are more often in precarious work situations than men, who are more likely to be in permanent, full-time, regular and better-paid jobs. "Permanent temporary employment" – characterized by successive short fixed-term contracts or fixed-term contracts with short breaks between them – is widely found among women workers. Women are also over-represented among home-based, casual and informal workers, and form the large majority of contributing family workers, often without pay.

Women and men engaged in precarious work are equally protected by the Conventions which protect fundamental rights and principles at work.

R. 198: Employment Relationship, 2006

➜ See also **Atypical work; Casual work; Part-time work; Social protection**

Public employment services and private employment agencies

Access to job opportunities is controlled by a wide range of agencies, including public employment services, private recruitment agencies, private or public counselling or placement services and vocational guidance institutions. These intermediate agents can play an important role in either promoting fairness or perpetuating discrimination in the labour market.

All public employment services and private employment agencies should promote equality of opportunity and treatment in access to employment and to particular occupations. For instance, questions put to job seekers should not try to elicit information that could result in discriminatory treatment or reduced access to employment. States shall ensure that private employment agencies treat workers without discrimination on the basis of race, colour, sex, religion, political opinion, national extraction, social origin or any other form of discrimination covered by national law and practice, such as age or disability.

The Private Employment Agencies Convention, 1997 (No. 181) and its accompanying Recommendation (No. 188) set out the principle of non-discrimination in the way such agencies treat workers and job seekers and draw up and publish vacancy notices or offers of employment. These instruments encourage private agencies to promote equality in employment through affirmative action programmes. The Convention also stipulates (Art. 11) that member States shall, in accordance with national law and practice, take the necessary measures to ensure adequate protection for the workers employed by private employment agencies as regards maternity protection and benefits, and parental protection and benefits. Art. 3 (e) of Convention No. 111 also covers non-discrimination in public services.

Special employment counselling modules adapted to the specific needs of women workers may be a useful tool to improve women's access to quality jobs.

> *C. 111: Discrimination (Employment and Occupation), 1958*
> *C. 181 and R. 188: Private Employment Agencies, 1997*
> *C. 160 and R. 170: Labour Statistics, 1985*

→ See also **Access to employment; Advertising for workers; Labour administration**

Public procurement policies

Public (or government) procurement policies can be a powerful device which governments can use to combat discrimination at work by setting equity-related criteria for winning public contracts. A pay equity policy or provision, for instance, can be made a prerequisite for companies aiming to secure a contract with a government. In Switzerland, the law on procurement obliges parties tendering for contracts to respect the principle of pay equity between men and women; while the South African Equity Act requires employers to possess a certificate stating that they respect equality in order to obtain government contracts. This is known as contract compliance.

→ See also **Equal remuneration**

R

Radiation protection

There is no special occupational radiation exposure limit for women in general, but in view of the particular health risks implied for women of child-bearing age and the possible greater sensitivity of the foetus to radiation, certain additional controls and precautions for pregnant workers may need to be considered.

The Radiation Convention, 1960 (No. 115) does not differentiate by sex in its provisions. However, the ILO's *Code of Practice on radiation protection of workers (Ionising radiations)*, published in 1986, includes pregnant women engaged in radiation work, alongside workers, students, apprentices and trainees between 16 and 18 years of age, in the categories of persons who may only work in conditions "where it is most unlikely that the annual exposure will exceed three-tenths of the dose limits".

The Recommendations of the International Commission on Radiological Protection (ICRP), issued in 1990, have a bearing on the application of Convention No. 115 in this respect, in so far as they have implications for "knowledge available at the time" and "current knowledge" (Art. 3 (1) and Art. 6 (2) of the Convention). The ICRP emphasizes that the employment of pregnant women should be of a type that does not carry a significant probability of high accidental radiation doses and intakes. As regards the protection of the unborn child, it recommends that where women of child-bearing age are engaged in work involving occupational exposure, the standard of protection provided for the unborn child should be broadly comparable with that required for members of the general public, and the mother's protection should be in line with this provision (ILO, 1992).[20] Employers should therefore make every reasonable effort to provide workers with suitable alternative employment in circumstances where it has been determined that a worker, for health reasons, may no longer continue in employment involving occupational exposure.

A woman worker should notify her employer as soon as possible on becoming aware that she is pregnant in order that her working conditions can be modi-

---

[20] See CEACR, General Observation concerning Convention No. 115, 1992.

fied, if necessary. The notification of pregnancy should not be considered a reason for discrimination or exclusion from work.

Exposure to radioactive sources can also harm men's reproductive function, potentially leading to sterility and mutagenic effects. Protective legislation that takes account of women's reproductive functions should therefore be extended to cover those of men.

Debate continues as to whether radiation from computer screens and printers is a significant risk to workers who use computers intensively.

> *C. 115 and R. 114: Radiation Protection, 1960*
> *R. 157: Nursing Personnel, 1977*
> *R. 194: List of Occupational Diseases, 2002*
> *International Basic Safety Standards for protection against ionizing radiation and for the safety of radiation sources, 1994*[21]

➜ See also **Computers; Health during maternity; Maternity protection; Occupational safety and health**

Remedies and sanctions

A remedy is a way of compensating a victim or correcting harm or damage suffered; a sanction is a criminal penalty or a civil administrative fine as a punishment for unacceptable behaviour. Both remedies and sanctions are ways of rendering the legal systems effective and of serving as a deterrent to illegal conduct. Remedies and sanctions are applied at the national level, often responding to calls in international labour standards for dissuasive measures in the most abhorrent areas of workforce abuse, such as in Forced Labour Convention, 1930 (No. 29), Art. 25, or Worst Forms of Child Labour Convention, 1999 (No. 182), Articles 7 (1) and 8.

National legislation on equal pay, opportunity and treatment is important, but is not by itself sufficient to ensure its application in law and practice. Discrimination should be prevented by effective means of deterrence, and victims of discrimination should be fairly compensated. In cases of unfair termination of employment, a monetary compensation is not generally regarded as sufficient. To secure acceptance of the law, it is important to have a range of remedies and/or sanctions available in instances of discrimination. As the nature of discrimination changes, becoming increasingly indirect, it becomes harder

---

[21] For more information, see: International Atomic Energy Agency (IAEA). 2003. *International Basic Safety Standards for protection against ionizing radiation and for the safety of radiation sources* (CD-ROM edition). Safety Series No. 115-1 (Vienna).

to address it through the use of criminal penalties alone; preventive measures are an increasingly necessary complement to sanctions for discriminatory behaviour.

A gradual trend towards strengthening remedies and sanctions can be observed. Most countries have established specialized and accessible bodies to tackle discrimination and promote equality at work; but many rely more heavily on sanctions than on remedies. For more effective enforcement, legal sanctions are combined with remedies in some countries. Remedies and sanctions are also becoming an increasingly important method of preventing and combating sexual harassment at the workplace.

Ombudspersons or ombud's offices are another way of investigating complaints and providing remedies. Typically, they make recommendations and assessments and submit an annual report to parliaments. They may be created especially to address equality issues and sensitive issues such as sexual harassment. Sweden, for instance, has an Equal Opportunities Ombud and an Equal Opportunities Commission: at the request of the Ombud, the Commission can order an employer to take specific measures to promote gender equality at work, under penalty of a fine for failure to comply.

→   See also **Disciplinary action; Discrimination; Grievance procedures; Harassment and pressure; Sexual harassment**

Remote working

Remote working is by no means coextensive with work in the ICT sector, but it emerged as a significant sector from the development of ICTs, as innovation in telecommunications made it much faster and cheaper to transfer data across borders, and it depends heavily upon computer use. It is part of the increasing flexibilization of the labour market, as the full-time jobs lost by computerization and automation in some sectors are replaced by flexible, part-time, frequently home-based jobs which can be done anywhere – not necessarily in the client's home country – and around the clock. Remote working is a very fast-growing sector and remote jobs have proven attractive to women workers in both the industrialized and developing countries.

Remote working is opening up opportunities for educated women in developing countries and countries distant from the advanced market economies to find employment opportunities in data processing, credit card billing centres and call centres. Jobs connected with the "information economy" were considered a window of opportunity for equal treatment and opportunity for women, since they came without the baggage of historical gender stereotyping. Even so, women workers are still under-represented in the information economy and tend to hold lower-skilled positions, for instance as data processors and call centre staff rather than computer programmers.

Teleworking can be defined as "distance work facilitated by information and communications technologies". Teleworkers can be home-based or can work in a group based in the same remote location, such as a call centre. These settings have some obvious advantages for women, and for this kind of work the workforce is predominantly female (ILO, 2002b, p. 127). In India, for example, where telework has grown very rapidly, some women work from home, especially where childcare facilities are non-existent or inadequate; but others prefer work in a call centre and regard it as empowering. Call centre work has also decreased the economic gender gap and enabled some young women to postpone marriage (Basi, 2006 and Coyle, 2006). Nonetheless, there are concerns about the health- and stress-related implications of repetitive work in high-pressure working environments. There are also obvious obstacles to association and organization by remote workers, especially those who are home-based.

Although the ILO does not yet have standards explicitly dealing with remote working, standards referring to home work, night work, and part-time work are applicable to different types of remote working. Measures should be taken to ensure that remote workers benefit from equality of treatment and conditions with those of comparable full-time workers as regards:

- protection against discrimination;

- maternity protection;

- remuneration;

- statutory social security protection;

- access to training;

- occupational safety and health (particularly referring to computer use);

- paid annual leave and paid public holidays;

- the right to organize;

- termination of employment.

In the European Union, the social partners signed a framework agreement on the regulation of telework in 2002, which covers areas such as employment conditions for teleworkers, health and safety, training and collective rights (Eurofound, 2007).

C. 171 and R. 178: Night Work, 1990
Protocol of 1990 to C. 89, Night Work (Women) (1948)
C. 175 and R. 182, Part-Time work, 1994

C. 177 and R. 184: Home Work, 1996
R. 198: Employment Relationship, 2006

→   See **Atypical work; Computers; Home-based work; Night work; Part-time workers; Work–life balance**

Representation and voice

In the current context of globalization, labour market fragmentation and dwindling of the State's role in social and economic development, mechanisms and institutions to ensure "voice" and representation for a wide spectrum of workers are strikingly absent. Agricultural workers and atypical workers of all kinds – including clandestine migrant workers – are denied freedom of association and the chance to exercise their right to the effective recognition of collective bargaining. Owners of micro-, small and medium-sized enterprises also come up against formidable barriers to membership of employers' organizations designed for larger businesses.

Since women form a large proportion, if not the majority, of workers in these situations, this lack of presentation and voice amounts to indirect discrimination. It is a crucial element of women's empowerment for women to have an equal voice with men at the highest levels of the instances of social dialogue. This can only be obtained through a more gender-balanced representation among the social partners. Equal participation in decision-making at these levels can lead to the introduction of more gender-equal legislation and policies on such issues as the balance between work and family, more equal access to decent work opportunities, and better social protection for women and men in informal and insecure work.

Trade unions are increasingly becoming aware of the necessity – and the benefit to themselves – of organizing and representing the interests of an increasingly multifaceted workforce. This requires a radical change in their organizing and alliance-building strategies, their institutional structures and the services they provide. They need to depart from their historical concept of the typical worker as a male breadwinner in regular, full-time employment, to reach out to unorganized workers and to learn from the forms of organizing undertaken by community groups, women's groups and others.

Employers' organizations, too, need to develop ways of representing SMEs and small businesswomen meaningfully. The business needs of women entrepreneurs are different from those of their male counterparts. The creation of women entrepreneurs' associations and women's cooperatives has often been an effective way of overcoming the discrimination women may face in setting up and running businesses.

> *C. 87: Freedom of Association and Protection of the Right to Organise, 1948*
> *C. 135: Workers' Representatives, 1971*
> *C. 154 and R. 163: Collective Bargaining, 1981*
> *R. 189: Job Creation in Small and Medium-Sized Enterprises, 1998*
> *R. 193: Promotion of Cooperatives, 2002*

➜ See also **Atypical work; Collective bargaining; Employers' organizations; Freedom of association and the right to organize; Social dialogue; Trade unions; Workers' organizations**

Retention of staff

➜ See **Diversity; Structural unemployment**

Rural workers

➜ See **Agricultural and rural workers**

S

Seasonal work

➜ See **Casual work**

Selection procedures

Selection procedures such as tests and interviews should be validated to ensure their relationship to the job. The place where tests and interviews are held should be in proximity to public transport and easily accessible.

The same tests and questions should be proposed to each applicant, without distinction of sex or any other attribute, and the responses should be evaluated on an objective basis by more than one person (preferably by persons of different sexes).

Pregnancy tests should never be carried out as part of employment selection procedures. Job applicants should not be required to disclose their marital status as part of a selection process.

> *C. 111 and R. 111: Discrimination (Employment and Occupation), 1958*
> *C. 183 and R. 191: Maternity Protection, 2000*

➜ See also **Access to employment; Discrimination; Marital status; Maternity protection**

Self-employed workers

Across legal systems a self-employed person is a worker who works independently of any single employer, in contrast to an employee or a dependent worker. Self-employed persons (also known as freelance, independent or own-account workers) provide services under contractual agreements for payment without any bonds of subordination to the contracting partner. The category of self-employed workers can be broken down further into self-employed workers with employees (those who are employers or entrepreneurs), self-employed workers without employees (own-account workers or sole traders), and members of producers' cooperatives.

Indicators for determining whether employment can be considered as self-employment vary across legal systems, but the primacy of the facts of the contractual arrangement is one common standard. Some member States use a general rebuttable presumption that all relationships involving one person's work for another in return for remuneration are employment relationships, and the parties must adduce evidence to prove that, on the contrary, they are self-employed. Recommendation No. 198 on the employment relationship states that national policies should provide guidance to employers and workers on establishing, among other things, the distinction between employed and self-employed workers

In practice, it is not always easy to distinguish self-employment from a disguised employment relationship. In order to avoid legal obligations linked with employment, a genuine employment relationship may be hidden as "self-employment", although the worker is in fact dependent (e.g. in the case of some homeworkers, who are primarily women). Such disguised employment should be governed by the law applicable to a "real" work relationship.

Self-employed workers are autonomous with respect to social security contributions. In practice, this often means that they are less protected by social security systems.

Self-employed workers are found in a wide range of occupations. A relatively high incidence of self-employment is characteristic of many developing countries. Worldwide, a growing number of women are engaging in own-account work, and women are now in the majority of some categories of self-employed persons. There are many reasons for this state of affairs. Some are "negative", including the "glass-ceiling" phenomenon (see p. 94), the gender pay gap, difficulty of access to (well-paid) jobs, and the need to reconcile economic activities with family responsibilities. Others are perhaps more positive and include the influence of support to women's entrepreneurship given by some governments.

Self-employed workers should enjoy the same fundamental rights as employees, though in practice it may be harder for them to access such rights because they lack representation and it is difficult for them to organize.

> *R. 169: Employment Policy (Supplementary Provisions), 1984*
> *C. 68: Employment Promotion and Protection against Unemployment, 1988*
> *R. 198: Employment Relationship, 2006*

→ See also **Access to employment; Cooperatives; Employee; Employment relationship; Equal remuneration; Glass ceiling; Home work; Informal economy; Older women workers; Women's entrepreneurship; Work–family balance**

Sexual harassment

Broadly speaking, sexual harassment in the workplace is any unwelcome sexual advances or verbal or physical conduct of a sexual nature, acceptance of which is explicitly or implicitly made a condition for favourable decisions affecting one's employment, or which has the purpose or effect of unreasonably interfering with the individual's work performance or creating an intimidating, hostile, abusive or offensive working environment. Sexual harassment may consist of:

- insults, remarks, jokes and insinuations of a sexual nature and inappropriate comments on a person's dress, physique, age or family situation;

- undesired and unnecessary physical contact such as touching, caresses, pinching or assault;

- embarrassing remarks and other verbal harassment;

- lascivious looks and gestures associated with sexuality;

- compromising invitations;

- requests or demands for sexual favours;

- explicit or implied threats of dismissal, refusal of promotion, etc. if sexual favours are not granted. [22]

Sexual harassment is considered to be a violation of human rights, a form of discrimination, and a safety and health issue. It offends the dignity and personal integrity of workers and calls into question their individual integrity and well-being. It also undermines their right to equal opportunity and treatment. It should be prevented in the workplace; where it occurs despite all efforts, it should be punished and the victims protected. The victims are often unaware of their rights and afraid of retaliation or of losing their jobs, so awareness-raising is an important element of the fight against sexual harassment.

Sexual harassment is a potential threat not only to workers but also to enterprises. It is recognized as contrary to the objectives of employers, since it weakens the basis upon which industrial relations are built and potentially has a negative effect on productivity, for instance through absenteeism, staff turnover and low staff morale. It can also tarnish a firm's public image and ultimately decrease its profits both through bad publicity and high litigation costs. The role of trade unions and employers in creating a healthy environment for the dignity of workers is of vital importance for prevention.

---

[22] For a more detailed list, see Chappell and di Martino, 2006, pp. 18–9.

Policies and procedures to eliminate sexual harassment should include:

- a policy statement;

- a complaint procedure adapted to sexual harassment that is confidential and provides protection from retaliation;

- progressive disciplinary rules;

- a training, awareness-raising and communication strategy.

The 71st session of the International Labour Conference in 1985 adopted a resolution on equal opportunities and equal treatment for men and women in employment which states that "sexual harassment at the workplace is detrimental to employee's working conditions and to employment and promotion prospects. Policies for the advancement of equality should therefore include measures to combat and prevent sexual harassment." (ILO, 1985, p. 91 as cited in ILO, 1988, p. 104)

Protection against sexual harassment is accorded in many countries under the constitution, equal opportunities or labour law, the penal code and/or specific legislation. The courts and tribunals at national level are in many cases further developing the role of employers in preventing harassment and dealing with its consequences through case law (dealing with termination of work contracts, remedies and sanctions, etc.) (Hodges-Aeberhard, 1996). Labour inspection services have an important role to play in hearing complaints or detecting sexual harassment in the workplace. Some employers' organizations favour the use of voluntary codes of conduct to counter sexual harassment (ILO, Bureau for Employers' Activities 2005, pp. 12 and 43).

Sexual harassment has been dealt with by the Committee of Experts on the Application of Conventions and Recommendations as a human rights issue, notably as an issue of discrimination against women, although men can also be targets. Other ILO activity to date has concentrated chiefly on research, drafting of legislation, and training and awareness-raising seminars, particularly in Asia and the Caribbean. More work is needed to broaden geographical coverage and to develop technical cooperation activities that will equip ILO constituents with instruments to address this form of discrimination more effectively.

C. 81: Labour Inspection, 1947
C. 111 and R. 111: Discrimination (Employment and Occupation), 1958
C. 169: Indigenous and Tribal Peoples, 1989

➜ See also **Discrimination; Harassment and pressure; Remedies and sanctions**

Sexual orientation

Sexual orientation may be very broadly defined as a preference for sexual partners of either the same or the opposite sex, or for both sexes. It is one of the
more recently recognized bases for discrimination. The prohibition of all discrimination based on sexual orientation should include male and female homo-
sexuals, bisexuals and heterosexuals, as well as transsexuals, transgendered persons and transvestites. Discrimination on the grounds of sexual orientation is
likely to form an element in multiple or composite discrimination, insofar as
someone who is homosexual or transgendered is more likely to be vulnerable
to sex discrimination as well. Bullying and harassment of people whose sexual
orientation is viewed stereotypically as "abnormal" is also a common feature of
discrimination against such people.

Sexual orientation is not a criterion provided for specifically in Convention
No. 111, but it is implicitly covered by Article 1.1 (b), which allows for member
States to extend the prohibited grounds for discrimination as they emerge. Some
States have determined that the criterion of sex includes sexual orientation.

Several countries have identified sexual orientation as a basis for discrimination
and opposing it. Some national and state constitutions (e.g. Germany, South
Africa) expressly prohibit discrimination on the grounds of sexual orientation,
and numerous others have addressed it in legislation in a variety of ways.
Nonetheless, in many parts of the world there is still strong resistance even to
recognizing sexual orientation as a cause for concern about discrimination.

> *C. 111: Discrimination (Employment and Occupation), 1958*
> *R. 188: Private Employment Agencies, 1997*

> ➜ *See also* **Discrimination; Harassment and pressure**

Shift work

➜ See **Hours of work; Night work**

Sick leave

Research suggests that differences in education, socialization and upbringing
generate differences in the way men and women manage illness and consequently in their use of sick leave provisions (Messing and Östlin, 2006, p. 20).
The types of employment relationship in which women and men respectively

predominate also influence patterns of sick leave take-up. Since women are strongly represented in atypical work, it is important, therefore, that several ILO labour standards (e.g. Convention No. 175 on part-time work, Recommendation 184 on home work) stipulate that sick leave for various categories of atypical worker should not be below the pro-rata level for full-time permanent workers, with money entitlements being determined in proportion to hours of work and earnings. Sick leave must also not entail any reduction in job security for any worker. Employers, in consultation with workers and their representatives, should take measures to reasonably accommodate workers with AIDS-related illnesses, including flexible sick leave (ILO, 2001a, p. 8).

A related provision is that of sickness benefit. Under the Medical Care and Sickness Benefit Convention, 1969 (No. 130), sickness benefit shall be offered to employees in the event of incapacity for work resulting from sickness and involving suspension of earnings, as defined by national legislation. The period over which sickness benefit is paid is normally 26 weeks from the first day of suspension of earnings.

When referring to women, sick leave and sickness benefit often seem to be confused or conflated with maternity leave and benefits. However, it is inappropriate to equate pregnancy and maternity leave with illness and sick leave, unless pregnancy or maternity presents complications leading to illness. Some countries' social security laws, rather than providing for specific maternity benefits, provide that during maternity leave, a worker will be entitled to sickness or unemployment benefits. However, treating maternity as a disability or the leave as a period of unemployment could be considered unequal treatment since, in general, such benefits are only available during a certain period, and women who use them in connection with maternity may find they do not have enough leave or benefits left to cover actual sickness or unemployment periods later. When the European Pregnant Workers Directive was being drafted in 1992, it was argued that in terms of equal treatment between men and women, maternity needed to be recognized as independent grounds for obtaining benefits (Séguret, 1997).

On the other hand, it is extremely important for women to have access to sick leave additional to their maternity leave in the event that they do suffer medical complications and health problems as a result of pregnancy or giving birth. Several important decisions by the European Court of Justice have confirmed that failure to allow a woman to take sick leave because her sickness is pregnancy-related constitutes unlawful sex discrimination. The European Pregnant Workers Directive allows for a woman to postpone her return to work for up to four weeks after the end of her maternity leave if she is ill.

Menstruation and menopause are among other sex-specific issues for women workers which may raise issues around sick leave. These are not in themselves illnesses but can be debilitating and can severely (if temporarily) reduce a woman's capacity for work. The menstrual cycle may be disturbed by a variety of conditions (such as amenorrhoea, menorrhagia, dysmenorrhoea, premenstrual syndrome and menopause) which may cause discomfort or concern for the employee. These may lead her to take regular sick leave, often reporting some other minor ailment rather than a menstrual problem, especially if the absence certificate is to be submitted to a male manager. Referral to a qualified health professional may resolve the problem rapidly (Last, 1997).

Where there are no provisions for workers to deal with emergencies, e.g. leave to care for sick children, workers may tend to explain their absences on more acceptable grounds, such as sick leave; and since women assume most of such care, their apparent high use of sick leave may be construed as reinforcing negative stereotypes about women's reliability as workers. Nonetheless, this disguised use of sick leave is quite common. In Australia, this has been recognized by the introduction of a principle of family or carer's leave, which enables employees to use their sick leave to care for sick family members (spouses, children, parents, grandparents or grandchildren) (ILO, 2004b). Such a provision is potentially significant for the carers of people with HIV/AIDS.

> R. 84: Labour Clauses (Public Contracts), 1949
> C. 111 and R. 111: Discrimination (Employment and Occupation), 1958
> R. 112: Occupational Health Services, 1959
> C. 149 and R. 157: Nursing Personnel, 1977
> C. 156 and R. 165: Workers with Family Responsibilities, 1981
> C. 175: Part-Time Work, 1994
> R. 184: Home Work, 1996

➜ See also **Domestic workers; HIV/AIDS; Home work; Illness in the family, leave for; Maternity leave; Nursing personnel; Part-time work**

Sickness insurance

➜ See **Health insurance**

Small and medium-sized enterprises

Many small and medium-sized enterprises (SMEs) particularly in developing countries are run by women, and Recommendation No. 189 on job creation in SMEs, notes that SMEs are a good channel of access to employment for women. But this does not necessarily mean that SMEs consciously promote gender equality or are run in a gender-sensitive way. Given their smaller resources, SMEs are even less likely than large companies to have equal opportunity policies in place or mechanisms for measuring their impact. ILO research in the Caribbean in 2001 found that the smaller the enterprise, the less likely it was to have a formal equal opportunities policy (ILO, 2003, p. 109).

Moreover, the fact that a SME has a formal policy does not mean that it will necessarily be translated into practice, although the existence of a policy does increase the possibility of equality in practice. SMEs usually cite limited human and financial resources and assumed relations of trust between workers and owner/managers in a small structure as reasons for these discrepancies.

Advocacy and capacity building needs to promote equity as regards power and voice at all levels between:

- small and large enterprises;

- female and male small entrepreneurs;

- women and men workers in SMEs.

Many projects promoting gender equality in SMEs focus mainly on encouraging women's entrepreneurship and the acquisition of skills. Equally important is advice to SMEs on practising equality of opportunity and treatment within their own workforces, so as to persuade them of the benefits of being equal opportunities employers.

Recommendation No, 189 recommends that member States should consider implementing various support services to enhance the growth and competitiveness of SMEs, such as the provision of "assistance in understanding and applying labour legislation, including provisions on workers' rights, as well as in human resources development and the promotion of gender equality" (Art. 11 (k)). Workers and employers' organizations should consider "participating in activities to ... promote ethical standards, gender equality and non-discrimination" (Art. 17 (h)).

The ILO's WEDGE (Women's Entrepreneurship Development and Gender Equality) programme plays a key role in ensuring that all the ILO's work on SMEs mainstreams important gender equality issues and documents good practices in this field.

R. 189: Job Creation in Small and Medium-Sized Enterprises, 1998

➜ See also **Women's entrepreneurship**

Social dialogue

Social dialogue, as defined by the ILO, includes all types of negotiation, consultation or simply exchange of information between or among representatives of governments, employers and workers, on issues of common interest relating to economic and social policy. It can be a tripartite process, with the government as an official party to the dialogue, or it can consist of bipartite relations between labour and management (or trade unions and employers' organizations) only, with or without indirect government involvement. Concertation can be informal or institutionalized, and often it is a combination of the two. It can take place at the national, regional or at enterprise level. It can be inter-professional or sectoral or a combination of these.

The main goal of social dialogue itself is to promote the building of consensus and democratic involvement among the main stakeholders in the world of work. Successful social dialogue structures and processes have the potential to resolve important economic and social issues, encourage good governance, including equality and equity, advance social and industrial peace and stability and boost economic progress.

Social dialogue echoes the needs and aspirations of its constituents. Its relevance depends on whether all segments of society can make their voices heard. The relatively small number of women in key positions in representative bodies acts as a brake on the advancement of gender equality in general and on improving the situation of both women and men in the world of work. Issues such as sex discrimination, equal pay, the reconciliation of work and family responsibilities (including childcare and elder care), working time arrangements, and sexual harassment will be adequately included on the social dialogue agenda only if a critical mass of women is participating actively and meaningfully in the dialogue and has access to decision-making roles in the social dialogue process There is therefore a pressing need to increase the participation of women in existing social dialogue structures, including unions and employers organizations, and have the gender dimension mainstreamed in the social dialogue agenda.

The desirability of equitable representation of women and men in the instances of social dialogue is suggested (though not made explicit) in two Conventions. Convention No. 87 specifies that workers and employers have the right to organize "without distinction whatsoever" (Art. 2). Convention No. 154 states that "bodies and procedures for the settlement of labour disputes should be so conceived as to contribute to the promotion of collective bargaining" (Art. 5.2 (e)); this should include gender-equitable representation if it is accepted that gender equality is crucial to such promotion.

These provisions open up opportunities for advocating gender equality in the application of the standards relevant to social dialogue, which can be promoted by ensuring that the voices of both men and women are heard in the representative instances of collective bargaining and tripartite negotiations and consultation, such as those suggested in the Tripartite Consultation Recommendation, 1976 (No. 152), (Para. 2 (3)). Existing good practices include the promotion of gender equality in a tripartite labour advisory body in Malawi, where at least one woman must, by law, be appointed to represent each of the tripartite constituents (ILO, 2004f, p. 8).

> *C. 87: Freedom of Association and Protection of the Right to Organise, 1948*
> *C. 98: Right to Organise and Collective Bargaining, 1949*
> *C. 144: Tripartite Consultation (International Labour Standards), 1976*
> *R. 152: Tripartite Consultation (Activities of the International Labour Organisation), 1976*
> *C. 154 and R. 163: Collective Bargaining, 1981*

→ See also: **Collective bargaining; Employers' organizations; Freedom of association and the right to organize; Representation and voice; Tripartism; Tripartite consultation; Workers' organizations**

Social pacts

→ See **Dismissal**

Social protection

Social protection is "the provision of a generalized basic social support for all citizens, regardless of contribution or employment history". This entails, for instance, income support to individuals on the basis of need rather than acquired rights, and health care for the entire population.

Access to an adequate level of social protection, as a basic, universal right of all individuals, is enshrined in both the Universal Declaration of Human Rights (1948) and the ILO's Declaration of Philadelphia (1944). This encompasses protection for the life and health of workers in all occupations, protection of child welfare and maternity, access to adequate nutrition and housing and equality in educational and vocational opportunities.

In practice, however, only 20 per cent of the world's population today enjoys access to adequate social protection, while more than half have none at all. While the process of globalization entails greater insecurity both for workers and employers and puts strong pressure on governments to cut public expenditure and businesses to reduce labour costs, social protection systems are confronting ageing populations (with life expectancy at retirement age increasing steadily by around 1.5 years every decade) and radical shifts in the organization of the labour market. In the industrialized countries, the challenge is to provide adequate protection in a situation of heightened uncertainty on the labour market while combating poverty and social exclusion in order to prevent sections of the population from being trapped in deprivation and exclusion. This means, first, designing new forms of protection better suited to workers' increasing mobility and, second, combining social inclusion policies with schemes guaranteeing a minimum income. In the developing countries, the traditional forms of protection formerly provided by the extended family and the community have largely become eroded in the processes of urbanization, industrialization and large-scale labour migration. Women's unpaid labour itself often ends up replacing social protection. There is an urgent need for new collective systems capable of protecting individuals who can no longer rely on traditional solidarity networks.

One of the ILO's key strategic objectives is to enable countries to extend social protection to all groups in society and to improve working conditions and safety and health at work. It aims to promote this by means of a set of tools, instruments and policies which aim, through government action and constant social dialogue, at ensuring that men and women enjoy, on an equal footing, decent working conditions which are safe, respect human dignity, take into account family and social values, allow for adequate compensation in case of lost or reduced income, permit access to adequate social and medical services and respect the right to free time and rest.

The different ways in which social protection is approached in developed and developing countries illustrate the need to take account of the diversity of national situations: for instance, whereas pensions may be the most pressing concern in countries with ageing populations, adequate healthcare provision is of higher priority in poor countries where life expectancy is lower, especially in the contexts of pandemics such as HIV/AIDS or malaria, or the ravages of conflict.

Informal economy workers are among the most numerous of those with little or no social protection, and women predominate in this sector. Most women in developing countries are engaged in some kind of informal work (Jhabvala and Sinha, 2006). Women workers in the informal economy are especially vulnerable to multiple risks because of their dual roles in the workplace and the home, their greater social exclusion, and the difficulty of extending social protection to them in a sector characterized by occupational diversity and geographical dispersion. Traditional mechanisms of social protection (e.g. kinship, care by children, local credit sources and savings groups, etc.) are not always effective, and often discriminate against women in any case. Social protection measures that will address these women need to cover a variety of issues – food, water, healthcare, childcare, shelter, and education. They can take the form of small-scale social insurance schemes, implemented through membership organizations for women. The Self-Employed Women's Association (SEWA) in India is an outstanding example of good practice in this respect through its comprehensive, contributory social insurance programme.

In particular, social protection must *not* be a way of imposing social choices that are a matter for national sovereignty and individual freedom. If, for instance, equality between men and women is a principle whose validity has been recognized by all the ILO's member countries, this *equality* is not to be seen as an *identity* of conditions. This means, for instance, that social security systems must respect the rights of women who have devoted all or part of their lives to work in the family rather than in the commercial sector.

> *C. 155 and R. 164: Occupational Safety and Health, 1981*
> *C. 156 and R. 165: Workers with Family Responsibilities, 1981*
> *C. 103: Maternity Protection (Revised) and R. 95: Maternity Protection, 1952*
> *C. 183 and R. 191: Maternity Protection, 2000*
> *MLC: Maritime Labour Convention, 2006*

➜ See also **Maternity protection; Occupational safety and health; Social security**

Social security

Social security can be conventionally defined as "the protection which society provides for its members against the economic and social distress that otherwise would be caused by the stoppage or substantial reduction of earnings resulting from sickness, maternity, employment injury, unemployment, invalidity, old age and death; the provision of medical care; and the provision of subsidies for families with children".

Minimum standards for all workers should be established in the following fields of social security:

* medical care;
* health insurance;
* unemployment benefit;
* pensions (old-age benefit);
* employment injury benefit;
* family benefit;
* maternity benefit;
* invalidity benefit;
* survivors' benefit.

Health insurance benefits, maternity protection and pensions concern all categories of workers employed in industrial and agricultural jobs, including women wage-earners working at home and domestic workers in private households. Social security benefits can be proportional to the beneficiary's earnings or family support commitment, set at uniform rates or linked to the means of the beneficiary concerned. The State has the general responsibility for the payment of the benefits and for the administration of the institution concerned.

The majority of social security systems were originally designed on the basis of the "male breadwinner model". This model was based on the assumption that it is the male as head of the family who earns the living, and the female who is primarily responsible for the unpaid care work. Married women were granted a form of protection derived from that enjoyed by the husband. Their earnings deriving from professional activity were regarded as supplementary. Current legislation still tends to reflect these origins, even if unequal treatment has been eliminated or greatly reduced in most industrialized countries.

The position of women, as well as attitudes towards family structures and roles, no longer corresponds to the traditional model. However, as a prevailing characteristic of many societies, women have no or reduced earnings for a number of years because of the unequal division of responsibilities for childcare and the household. Specifically in order to prevent poverty of widowed women in old age, women's access to and coverage by social security and pension schemes should be revised at the national level. Social security systems can try to:

- compensate for this unequal sharing of domestic tasks (e.g. by pension splitting); and

- encourage more equal sharing (e.g. by providing parental benefits, available to fathers and/or mothers).

At national and international levels, the following are areas of concern in the context of promoting equal treatment for men and women in matters of social security:

- the tailoring of rights to benefits and the "individualization" of such rights;

- equality of treatment as regards retirement age;

- equality of treatment as regards survivors' benefits;

- the division of pension rights in the event of separation; and

- taking into account the situation of parents with family responsibilities for the calculation of or access to benefits.

A resolution and conclusions concerning social security were adopted by the International Labour Conference at its 89th Session in 2001. These instruments adopted a broad, lifecycle-based concept of social protection from the standpoint of maintaining people's skills in the long term (in particular through initial education and lifelong learning), so as to maintain their employability. There is also a broad conception of the scope of application of social security. Linking social security to decent work helps to anchor it in the principles of dignity and solidarity. For instance, uncoupling the need for social security from work in employment in the strict sense means that positive account can be taken, over and above employment, of self-employment, work in the informal economy, and unpaid personal care work carried out chiefly by women. In this way social protection can reach those who need it most.

> *R. 29: Sickness Insurance, 1927*
> *C. 102: Social Security (Minimum Standards), 1952*
> *C. 118: Equality of Treatment (Social Security), 1962*
> *C. 157: Maintenance of Social Security Rights, 1982*
> *C. 103: Maternity Protection (Revised) and R. 95: Maternity Protection, 1952*
> *C. 183 and R. 191: Maternity Protection, 2000*

→   See also **Conditions and benefits of employment; Employment injury benefit; Maternity leave; Maternity protection; Pension (retirement benefit); Occupational segregation; Health insurance**

Stress

→   See **Computers; Occupational safety and health**

Structural unemployment

This term is used to describe unemployment caused by changes in the structure of the economy resulting from technological innovations or by changes in the composition of the labour force. In many countries women are often among the first to lose their jobs when structural changes of this kind take place, because the main breadwinners and heads of households are still assumed to be male. Structural unemployment also occurs when there is a mismatch between the education offered to males and females and the needs and opportunities presented by the labour market. In many countries, sex-based segregation in the curriculum can mean that the education of girls (but also in certain cases that of boys) does not lead to employment.

Employers should take particular care that any workers who must be made redundant are treated with strict equity in the definition of criteria and timetables for redundancy. It should never be assumed that women are less likely to be the chief or sole breadwinners in their families and would therefore be less adversely affected by redundancy.

Member States should identify human resources development, education, training and lifelong learning policies which emphasize, among other things, the gender-equitable development of competencies and job retention in the context of decent work. According to the level of economic development of the country, technology policies should contribute to improving working conditions and reducing hours of work, and should include measures to prevent job losses. These measures, aimed at the retention of staff, could include:

- retraining workers to meet the modified employment requirements resulting from technological change;

- involving workers and their representatives in the planning, introduction and use of new technologies;

- improving the organization of working time, with an aware of the need to safeguard work–family balance, to create new employment opportunities, on a gender-equitable basis, while increasing productivity and satisfying the basic needs of the population.

C. 168: Employment Promotion and Protection against Unemployment, 1988
R. 169: Employment Policy (Supplementary Provisions), 1984
R. 195: Human Resources Development, 2004

➡ See also **Employment policy and promotion; Female-headed households; Human resources development; Non-traditional occupations; Work–family balance**

Survivors' benefit

All persons protected under social security systems should be entitled to survivors' benefit. Benefits should accrue to both widows and widowers. A woman or man who was maintained by her or his spouse at the time of death, or children that suffer the loss of support following the death of the insured worker, should be entitled to a periodical payment. The right of the widow or widower may be conditional on his or her incapacity for self-support, and the benefit may be reduced or suspended if the person is engaged in gainful activity. This benefit may also be conditional upon a minimum period of contribution or employment. If a surviving spouse has no child and is presumed to be incapable of self-support, evidence of a minimum duration of the marriage may be required.

C. 102: Social Security (Minimum Standards), 1952
C. 128 and R. 131: Invalidity, Old Age and Survivors' Benefits, 1967

➡ See also **Social protection; Social security**

T

Teachers

The teaching profession is one where women have traditionally been employed, but are nevertheless concentrated in more junior positions. The joint ILO/ UNESCO Recommendation concerning the status of teachers adopted in 1966 is still authoritative as an instrument to promote good practice in teaching. It emphasizes that all aspects of the preparation and employment of teachers should be free from any form of discrimination on grounds of race, colour, sex, religion, political opinion, national or social origin, or economic condition (Para. III.7). According to this Recommendation:

- Marriage should not be considered a bar to the appointment or to the continued employment of women teachers, nor should it affect remuneration or other conditions of work;

- Employers should be prohibited from terminating contracts of service for reasons of pregnancy and maternity leave;

- Arrangements such as crèches or nurseries should be considered where desirable to take care of the children of teachers with family responsibilities;

- Measures should be taken to permit women teachers with family responsibilities to obtain teaching posts in the vicinity of their homes and to enable married couples, both of whom are teachers, to teach in the same general neighbourhood or in the same school;

- In appropriate circumstances, women teachers with family responsibilities who have left the profession before retirement age should be encouraged to return to teaching;

- Part-time service should be facilitated: part-time working teachers should receive proportionately the same remuneration and enjoy the same basic conditions of employment as teachers employed on a full-time basis, should be granted corresponding rights and should be entitled to adequate and appropriate social security protection, including coverage under employers' pension schemes;

- Effect should be given to the standards laid down in the Convention No. 3 and Convention (No. 103 on maternity protection;[23]

---

[23] The Maternity Protection Convention, 2000 (No. 183) updates these instruments.

- Women teachers with children should be encouraged to remain in the service by such measures as enabling them, at their request, to take additional unpaid leave of up to one year after childbirth without loss of employment, all rights resulting from employment being fully safeguarded.

The Joint ILO-UNESCO Committee of Experts on the Application of the Recommendation concerning the Status of Teachers (CEART) was set up to oversee implementation of the Recommendation. Among its tasks is the examination of allegations from teachers' organizations on non-observance of the Recommendation's provisions in member States. After considering the content of an allegation, CEART issues its findings and makes recommendations for the resolution of the problems or conflict. CEART's 2006 report contains a section on gender in education. [24]

The UNESCO Recommendation concerning the Status of Higher-Education Teaching Personnel complements the 1966 Recommendation. It was adopted in 1997, following years of preparatory work by UNESCO and the ILO, and refers to the ILO's standards on freedom of association and the right to organize, collective bargaining, and equality of opportunity and treatment.

> *Joint ILO/UNESCO Recommendation concerning the Status of Teachers, 1966*
> *UNESCO Recommendation concerning the Status of Higher-Education Teaching Personnel, 1997*

→ See also **Family responsibilities, workers with; Maternity protection; Occupational segregation; Vocational training**

Teleworking

→ See **Remote working**

Termination of employment

→ See **Dismissal**

---

[24] For more information, see http://www.ilo.org/public/english/standards/relm/gb/docs/gb298/pdf/ceart-10.pdf.

Trade unions, gender equality in

Trade unions or workers' organizations are established for protecting and/or improving, through collective action, the economic and social situation of workers of both sexes. The right to form and join trade unions without discrimination is guaranteed by Conventions Nos. 87 and 98. Together with governments and employers' organizations, they make up the tripartite constituent structure of the ILO which engages in social dialogue.

Trade unions, their representatives and members should ensure respect for and promotion of equal remuneration, opportunity and treatment through their relations with management. Like employers' organizations, trade unions have a prime responsibility to identify and recognize discriminatory practice and to combat it through all their activities, starting within their own organizations.

In this regard, they should engage in the following equal opportunity and treatment policies:

- encouraging management to introduce adequate measures in areas where they do not exist, and negotiating the extension of existing policies;

- negotiating for the inclusion in collective bargaining agreements of clauses on equal opportunities, protection against discrimination, affirmative action and family-friendly arrangements;

- cooperation with and assistance to management in formulating, implementing and monitoring equal opportunity and treatment policies.

Within the trade union organization, representatives and members should ensure equal opportunities and treatment and sex-balanced representation. In particular, the presence of a critical mass of women in decision-making positions in trade unions is key for promoting gender equality in the world of work. In this respect, trade unions should:

- solicit membership from workers of all groups and both sexes in the workplace; this may include positive action measures to promote the affiliation of women;

- encourage the election of representatives from the under-represented sex and under-represented groups; special measures should be taken to guarantee women's equal sharing of decision-making;

- encourage all workers to participate in union activities, particularly in education and training, which are aimed at increasing awareness and capacity building to promote equality;

- provide information to all members on their equal role in the union, union procedures and structure, and their rights and responsibilities under collective bargaining agreements, relevant laws and other legal provisions and work rules;

- provide support to members alleging discrimination in the workplace, in the form of guidance, educational activities, information and, where appropriate, representation.

Although union membership as a proportion of the workforce has declined in most countries, the proportion of union members who are women is rising in many places. This is encouraging, for it has been widely recognized that trade unions are on the whole still very male-dominated and operate according to long-standing masculine priorities, schedules and organizational cultures. However, the trade union movements in a number of countries have recognized that their continued survival and strength demand that they undertake activities relevant to the needs of the changing workforce, and more particularly, working parents, women and workers in female-dominated sectors, such as part-timers.

> *C. 87: Freedom of Association and Protection of the Right to Organise, 1948*
> *C. 98: Right to Organise and Collective Bargaining, 1949*
> *C. 141: Rural Workers' Organisations, 1975*
> *C. 151: Labour Relations (Public Service), 1978*

➜ See also **Collective bargaining; Employers' organizations; Family responsibilities, workers with; Freedom of association and the right to organize; Fundamental principles and rights at work; Representation and voice; Social dialogue; Tripartism; Tripartite consultation**

Trafficking in persons

The Protocol to Prevent, Suppress and Punish Trafficking in Persons, Especially Women and Children (the Trafficking Protocol or Palermo Protocol), supplementing the United Nations Convention against Transnational Organized Crime, adopted in 2000, defines trafficking in persons:

> the recruitment, transportation, transfer, harbouring or receipt of persons, by means of the threat or use of force or other forms of coercion, of abduction, of fraud, of deception, of the abuse of power or of a position of vulnerability or of the giving or receiving of payments or benefits to achieve the consent of a person having control over another person, for the purpose of exploitation. Exploitation shall include, at a minimum, the exploitation of the prostitution of others or other forms of sexual exploitation, forced labour or services, slavery or practices similar to slavery, servitude or the removal of organs (Art. 3 (a)).

However, the Protocol defines child trafficking differently: where the victim is a girl or boy under 18 years of age, their "recruitment, transportation, transfer, harbouring or receipt for the purpose of exploitation" is considered human trafficking even if this does not involve any of the illicit means mentioned above (coercion, abduction, deception, etc.) (Art. 3 (c) and (d)).

Trafficking is very closely linked to forced labour. It can occur both within single country's territory as well as between neighbouring or distant countries. The estimated minimum number of persons in forced labour at a given time as a result of trafficking is 2.45 million (ILO, 2005b, p. 14, para. 56). It has also been estimated that children represent 40–50 per cent of all trafficking victims (ILO, 2005b, p. 15, para. 61). According to a 2003 report by an EU-convened Expert Group on Trafficking in Human Beings, forced labour is the "crucial element" of the Trafficking Protocol, and efforts to combat trafficking should concentrate on the forced labour exploitation of trafficked persons rather than on the mechanisms of trafficking itself.

Trafficking in persons for exploitative labour, and especially for forced commercial sexual exploitation, affects women and girls disproportionately. While accurate estimates are hard to arrive at, it is clear that women and girls are the majority of trafficked persons in the world. Men and boys are also trafficked for particular purposes, for instance in Brazil, where male workers are trafficked within the country to large cattle ranches or logging camps. Trafficking is related in part to women's unequal access to decent work as a result of sex discrimination in the labour market, as well as to traditional beliefs that devalue women and girls. People who are subject to racial and gender discrimination are often also victims of trafficking.

Several States parties to the Trafficking Protocol have adopted new anti-trafficking laws, although some of them cover only the sexual exploitation of women and children. However, states are increasingly seeking to broaden their definition of trafficking to encompass forced labour exploitation as well.

While there is no specific ILO Convention dealing with trafficking in persons, the ILO focuses on the labour aspects of trafficking and on the linkages between trafficking and forced labour, child labour, migration, and discrimination. The ILO's action against human trafficking is based on a number of relevant standards on forced and child labour, the protection of migrant workers, equality of rights, employment services and employment policy (ILO, 2005b, p. 69, box 3.1). For instance, ILO supervisory bodies have regularly dealt with forced prostitution and sexual exploitation under Convention No. 29 as well as Convention No. 182.

Most recently, the Recommendation No. 198 refers to the need for member States to prevent abuses against migrant workers "who may be affected by uncertainty as to the existence of an employment relationship" (Para. 7(a)).

Where workers are recruited in one country to work in another, bilateral agreement may be considered to prevent "abuses and fraudulent practices which have as their purpose the evasion of the existing arrangements for the protection of workers in the context of an employment relationship" (Art. 7 (b)). These measures focused on the employment relationship could be added to comprehensive action against human trafficking.

The UN Commission on the Status of Women adopted a Resolution, *Eliminating Demand for Trafficked Women and Girls for All Forms of Exploitation*, in 2005.

> *C. 29: Forced Labour, 1930*
> *C. 143: Migrant Workers (Supplementary Provisions), 1975*
> *C. 182 and R. 190: Worst Forms of Child Labour, 1999*
> *R. 198: Employment Relationship, 2006*

➜   See also **Child labour; Forced labour; Migrant workers**

Tripartism

Tripartism is the process of cooperation between governments, employers' organizations and workers' organizations – the constituents of the ILO – in decision-making in the sphere of competence of the ILO. The tripartite constituents are the primary agents for promoting equality at work.

All Conventions and Recommendations are drawn up by representatives of governments, employers and workers and adopted at the International Labour Conference; thus the authority of the international labour standards derives from tripartite involvement in their formulation and applications.

The prerequisite for tripartism, the freedom of association and right to organize, as enshrined in Conventions No. 87 and No. 98, are fundamental principles aiming at the free exercise of the rights of workers and employers.

Three key instruments promote tripartism: the Tripartite Consultation Convention, 1976 (No. 144), its associated Recommendation No. 152, and Consultation (Industrial and National Levels) Recommendation, 1960 (No. 113). Of these, Recommendation No. 113 specifies that measures to promote effective consultation and cooperation at the industrial and national levels between public authorities and employers' and workers' organisations should be applied without discrimination against these organizations or amongst them on grounds such as the race, sex, religion, political opinion or national extraction of their members. The 2002 ILC Resolution on tripartism and social dialogue emphasizes the importance of seeking sex balance in delegations to ILO bodies. The International Labour Office is mandated to report formally on the numbers of women and men participating not only in major fora such as the International Labour Conference but also in tripartite events at the regional and project level.

Tripartite partnerships at the national level have strong potential to promote gender equality. An important prerequisite, however, is the representation of both women and men on as equitable a basis as possible in the participating tripartite bodies. To date, however, an equitable balance of representation between men and women has not been achieved in any tripartite structure; all these structures are dominated by men. Research to establish baseline data on women's participation in social dialogue institutions carried out in 2006 by the ILO's Social Dialogue, Labour Law and Labour Administration department (DIALOGUE) found that in 48 bipartite, tripartite and "tripartite-plus" bodies worldwide, an average of 14.7 per cent of the participants were women. Government representations had the highest level of female participation, employers the lowest. Strategies to improve gender balance in social dialogue institutions should focus on promoting women in managerial positions in social partners' organizations, the public administration and government.

→   See also **Employers' organizations; Tripartite consultation; Workers' organizations**

Tripartite consultation

Tripartite consultation is an advisory process which aims to help governments take decisions about matters related to ILO standards and to ensure that the voices of the social partners – workers' and employers' organizations – will be heard by the government before decisions are taken. It is not a negotiation process intended to lead to agreement, like that involved in the tripartite drafting of standards.

Convention No. 144 calls for effective consultation between government, employers' and workers' representatives at each stage of ILO standards-related activities, from setting the agenda of the International Labour Conference to ratification and denunciation of standards. The associated Recommendation No. 152 suggests other related issues on which consultation could take place, such as technical cooperation, resolutions and conclusions of ILO meetings, and the promotion of better knowledge of ILO activities. Gender equality could be mainstreamed into many of these areas. A number of other conventions, for example those regarding minimum wage fixing, private employment agencies and the worst forms of child labour, envisage consultation between government, workers' and employers' organizations in their implementation.

Tripartite consultation can thus be used to promote awareness of discrimination and the need for equality between men and women at work. In many countries advisory and promotional bodies, including national commissions on women or equality, have been set up for this purpose. Their structure is usually "tripartite-plus", allowing for the inclusion of representatives of the main stakeholder groups in civil society.

The parties to tripartite consultation can ensure that the voices of both women and men are heard during consultations, by promoting the balanced representation of both women and men in the consultative bodies and the inclusion of issues of specific concern to women and to men. National women's machineries and women's sections of trade union confederations can be included among the consultative bodies mentioned in Recommendation No. 152, Para. 2 (3) (b). When a new body is created in the context of tripartite consultation, or where one already exists, provision can be made for it to be gender-balanced. Training for participants in the consultation process should be offered to women and men on an equal basis, and where women are underrepresented, positive training and other measures can be considered to boost women's participation.

Points relevant to gender equality can be discussed in the context of the consultations. The process can also pay particular attention to the ratification and implementation of gender-relevant ILO standards.

> *R. 113: Consultation (Industrial and National Levels), 1960*
> *C. 144: Tripartite Consultation (International Labour Standards), 1976*
> *R. 152: Tripartite Consultation (Activities of the International Labour Organisation), 1976*
> *Articles 19 and 22 of the Constitution of the International Labour Organisation*

→   See also **Representation; Social dialogue; Tripartism**

U

Underemployment

A person is defined as underemployed according to the ILO's understanding of the term if he or she is employed but expresses a wish to work more with a correspondingly higher remuneration, and is available to take up an extended employment within two weeks of expressing that wish. Time-related underemployment, as used in the ILO's labour market database, *Key Indicators of the Labour Market (KILM)*, is a measure indicating that the hours of work an employed person is doing are fewer than that person is willing and available to take. Like other aspects of employment, underemployment has a gender dimension and sex-disaggregated statistics on underemployment should be collected and analysed.

➤ See also **Employment-intensive works programmes; Employment policy; Informal economy; Labour statistics; Unemployment; Youth employment**

Underground work

➤ See **Mines**

Unemployment

Unemployed people are defined as all persons above a specified age who, during a recent brief reference period (usually a week or two), were without work, currently available for work and seeking work of at least one hour's duration (ILO, 2006a, p. ix, note 3). This definition does not measure the underemployment that is endemic in the informal economy in many countries, particularly developing countries.

Although women's employment rates have risen consistently in most countries over the past decades, women almost everywhere are unemployed and underemployed to a greater extent than men. As a result of their traditionally larger share of responsibilities for childcare and the household, women also face more difficulties in being immediately available for work and rely more heavily on atypical and flexible forms of work for an income.

Unemployment benefit is a periodical payment which should be made in case of suspension of earnings due to inability to obtain suitable employment for a person capable of, and available for, work. The duration of the benefit should vary according to the category of employment and the length of the contribution period.

A woman's marital status (including common-law unions) should not carry any weight in assessing her qualification for receiving unemployment benefit.

> *C. 102: Social Security (Minimum Standards), 1952*
> *C. 168: Employment Promotion and Protection against Unemployment, 1988*

➜ See also **Marital status; Social security; Social protection**

Unemployment benefit

➜ See **Unemployment**

Unpaid work

The ILO includes unpaid work carried out in the family and community, often alongside paid work, in its understanding of work. Largely as a result of the recommendations of the Beijing Platform for Action emerging from the Fourth World Conference on Women (1995), there are now international guidelines for estimating the value of unpaid work, which recognize that unpaid work, most of which is carried out by women, has an economic value.

Estimating the value of unpaid work remains complex, however. Unpaid family workers, mostly women and children, make up a large proportion of the people working in the informal economy. Productive but unpaid work is often confused with household work. While estimation of the value of some kinds of unpaid work, for instance work carried out by family members contributing to a family enterprise, is included in national accounting in some countries, this is far less common with respect to unpaid care work in the family, which is largely invisible. In some countries the gender division of unpaid household labour is more unequal than in others.

However, valuing unpaid work is an important way of recognizing the usually unacknowledged economic contribution of the people who do it. When unpaid work is counted in, the differences in the measured contributions of men, women and children to the economy or their households are reduced.

Recommendation No. 165 on workers with family responsibilities recommends (Para. VII. 32) that the competent national authorities should promote such public and private action as is possible to lighten the burden deriving from the family responsibilities of workers, including adequate and affordable home-help and home-care services.

> *C. 111 and R. 111: Discrimination (Employment and Occupation), 1958*
> *R. 165: Workers with Family Responsibilities, 1981*

→ See **Atypical work; Care work; Casual work; Child labour; Division of labour; Economic activity; Employment-intensive works programmes; Equality of opportunity and treatment in employment and occupation; Housework; Occupational segregation; Older women workers; Social protection; Social security**

V

Violence at work, gender-based

Discrimination at work may be compounded by physical or psychological violence which may be gender-based. The clearest illustration of this is sexual harassment; but harassment accompanied by violence or the threat of violence need not be sexual in intent. Recent ILO research has identified female migrant domestic workers as a high-risk group in countries such as Saudi Arabia, for example. There is a close connection between violence at work and precarious work, gender, youth, and certain high-risk occupational sectors. A young woman with a precarious job in the hotel industry, for instance, is much more likely to be exposed to the risk of sexual harassment than a mature male office worker with a permanent job.

National and international legislation against workplace violence and gender-based violence exists, but preventive action is essential to create and sustain a violence-free working environment where women workers can feel as physically and psychologically as safe as their male colleagues.

Gender-based violence is a very complex issue, rooted in gendered power relations in the economy, the labour market, the employment relationship, organizational culture and cultural factors.

Workplace measures to combat gender-based violence may include:

*   regulations and disciplinary measures;

*   policy interventions against violence;

*   disseminating information about positive examples of innovative legislation, guidance and practice;

*   workplace designs that may reduce risks;

*   collective agreements;

*   awareness raising and training for managers, workers and government officials dealing with or exposed to violence at work;

*   designing and putting in place procedures to improve the reporting of violent incidents in conditions of safety and confidentiality.

In 2004, the ILO drew up a code of practice entitled *Workplace violence in services sectors and measures to combat this phenomenon.* The workplace violence and harassment programme of ILO's TRAVAIL department also addresses the prevention of all forms of workplace violence, including sexual harassment and violence. It not only conducts and commissions research on the nature and extent of workplace violence issues and on measures taken to address them, but also develops practical tools and offers advice to governments and workers' and employers' organizations on how to prevent and respond to violence at work. The ILO's Addressing Psychological Problems at Work programme (SOLVE) of the Programme on Safety and Health at Work and the Environment (SAFE-WORK) is an interactive educational programme designed to assist in the development of policy and action to address psychosocial issues at the workplace, including violence; see **Further resources.**

C. 111 and R. 111: *Discrimination (Employment and Occupation), 1958*

→   See also **Domestic workers; Harassment and pressure; Sexual harassment**

Vocational guidance

Vocational guidance aims to help individuals learn about opportunities for education, training, lifelong learning and work, and to facilitate their career planning. It includes vocational orientation and counselling, and may be given in schools, training centres, specialized offices or institutions.

Vocational guidance services can play an essential role in promoting equal opportunity for girls and women in their choice of jobs, vocational training courses and future occupational areas. They therefore need to be gender-sensitive. Such services ought to ensure that proposals are not influenced by considerations based on stereotypes or prejudices that have the effect of channelling women into particular sectors or activities.

C. 142: *Human Resources Development, 1975*
R. 195: *Human Resources Development, 2004*

→   See also **Education; Human resources development; Occupational segregation; Vocational training**

Vocational training

Vocational training comprises activities intended to provide the skills, knowledge, competencies and attitudes required for employment in a particular occupation, or a group of related occupations, in any field of economic activity. By equipping groups that are discriminated against with the skills needed to improve their employability, productivity and income, vocational training can play an important role in promoting equality of opportunities for all workers to obtain decent work.

Measures to promote equality of opportunity of women and men in training and employment should include:

- education for both men and women to encourage both sexes to play an equal role in changing traditional attitudes;

- vocational guidance enabling girls and women to take advantage of vocational training opportunities;

- widening the scope of the training beyond the traditionally "female" spheres (domestic science, needlework, cooking, care work, clerical/secretarial work, etc.);

- equal access for girls and women to all streams of education and vocational training for all types of occupations, and further training to ensure their personal development and advancement;

- daycare and other facilities for all workers with family responsibilities to allow their access to normal vocational training;

- vocational training programmes and lifelong learning for women and men who are above the normal age of entry into employment, and for those who wish to re-enter work after a break for child-rearing.

C. 111 and R. 111: Discrimination (Employment and Occupation), 1958
C. 142: Human Resources Development, 1975
R. 195: Human Resources Development, 2004

→ See also **Education; Human resources development; Occupational segregation; Vocational guidance**

W

White lead (painting)

➜ See **Chemicals**

Women in development

➜ See **Gender analysis and planning**

Women's empowerment

➜ See **Gender analysis and planning**

Women's entrepreneurship

In recent years, small and medium-sized enterprises (SMEs), including micro-enterprises, have become important sources of employment and self-employment for women in both developed and developing countries, and there has been a significant rise in the number of women entrepreneurs in a variety of economic activities in both the formal and informal economies. In many developing countries more women than men work in SMEs (ILO, 2004d, para. 391).

The SME sector is very diverse in terms of women entrepreneurs' motivation, socio-economic status, type of business and potential for growth. It covers everything from agricultural micro-enterprises to modern commercial and professional enterprises run on the internet. However, there is evidence that women's enterprises tend to be smaller both in terms of the number of workers employed and the presence and value of fixed assets. Women entrepreneurs tend to be concentrated in low-investment, less remunerative occupations derived from their traditional skills (such as selling in market stalls and small-scale food production and catering), while male entrepreneurs tend to be concentrated in more dynamic, investment-intensive areas. For both male and female small entrepreneurs, there is little security and high vulnerability to the vagaries of the market.

Women entrepreneurs often have to contend with policies and regulatory and institutional environments that are unfriendly to women. They tend to register their enterprises less frequently than men and often operate from the home. Being informal, such work tends to be penalized rather than regulated, particularly in developing countries. Many women, although self-employed, are not recognized – or do not recognize themselves – as entrepreneurs and thus are overlooked by institutions and programmes interested in enterprise development (ILO, 2004d, para. 388). Women are also under-represented in employers' organizations and business associations.

Women do not have the same access as men to finance, assets, technology or services, they often have relatively lower levels of education and vocational training, and they have to juggle the management of their business with their domestic responsibilities. In many agricultural societies, the fact that women cannot own or inherit the land they farm affects not only their ability to work independently as farmers but also their right to associate in cooperatives and credit unions.

While women entrepreneurs undoubtedly experience difficulties in running SMEs, many of which are gender-specific, it should be pointed out that many of the obstacles are generic. Women entrepreneurs may, however, experience these to an exaggerated degree.

The rights of self-employed people and owners of small and micro-enterprises, as well as those of their employees, are secured by generic equality legislation in many cases and are covered by ILO Conventions and Recommendations. However, gender equality issues need to be incorporated specifically into the legal and regulatory framework governing micro- and small enterprise development. Some standards do this. Recommendation No. 189, in particular, calls on member States to consider:

> "specific measures and incentives for persons aspiring to become entrepreneurs among selected categories of the population, such as women, long-term unemployed, persons affected by structural adjustment or restrictive and discriminatory practices, disabled persons, demobilized military personnel, young persons including graduates, older workers, ethnic minorities and indigenous and tribal peoples." (Recommendation No. 189, Para. 16 (4)).

In a specific provision (Para. 16), it asks member States to "encourage support for female entrepreneurship, recognizing the growing importance of women in the economy, through measures designed specifically for women who are or wish to become entrepreneurs." Such measures could address underlying inequalities in access to resources, vocational and business training and decision-making.

In the ILO, the Women's Entrepreneurship Development and Gender Equality (WEDGE) programme promotes women's entrepreneurship in the context of decent work. The WEDGE team is part of the ILO's Boosting Employment through Small Enterprise Development (SEED) programme. It works on enhancing economic opportunities for women by carrying out affirmative actions in support of women starting, formalizing and growing their enterprises. WEDGE's approach is based on developing the knowledge base on women entrepreneurs and gender inequalities in resources, access, needs and opportunities regarding SMEs; promoting representation, advocacy and voice, for instance by building the capacity of women entrepreneurs' associations; and developing innovative support services for women entrepreneurs, including training guides and tools.[25]

> *R. 189: Job Creation in Small and Medium-Sized Enterprises, 1998*

→   See **Access to employment; Education; Human resources development; Small and medium-sized enterprises; Vocational training**

Work–family balance

Motherhood and the gendered division of labour that places primary responsibility for maintaining the home and family on women are important determinants of gender-based inequalities between the sexes and of inequalities among women. Conflict between these family responsibilities and the demands of work contributes significantly to women's disadvantage in the labour market and the sluggish progress towards equal opportunity and treatment for men and women in employment. While women are forced, or choose, to accept poorly-paid, insecure, part-time, home-based or informal work in order to combine their family responsibilities with their paid employment, difficulties in reconciling the demands of work and family contribute to men's disadvantage in the family and limit their ability to be involved in family matters.

Workplace schedules that do not take into account workers' family responsibilities can constitute indirect discrimination in that they force such workers to "under-perform" in terms of participation in workplace activities and thus potentially damage their career development prospects. In particular, women's career advancement may suffer when they take a "career break" longer than the statutory maternity leave for the purposes of family care or take up parental leave provisions immediately after maternity leave.

---

[25] For full information on WEDGE, see http://www.ilo.org/dyn/empent/empent.Portal?p_prog=S&p_subprog=WE.

However, there has recently been an increasing recognition of the importance of devising measures to help reconcile workers' family responsibilities with their work – a key strategy to facilitate women's greater participation in decent work. As clearer links have been established between the achievement of equality between women and men at home and at the workplace, the issue of harmonizing employment and family commitments for both women and men has emerged as an important labour and social policy theme in a growing number of countries.

Convention No. 156 sees equality of opportunity as the overall objective of work–family measures. However, not all work–family measures promote equality. As noted in a recent ILO Global Report: "There is a danger that work/family policies, which are often aimed implicitly or explicitly at women in particular, may end up reinforcing the image of women as 'secondary earners' and accruing to the double burden of working women" (ILO, 2003, p. 77).

For a list of recommended actions to take to promote work–family balance, see *Family responsibilities, workers with* (p. 80).

> *C. 156 and R. 165: Workers with Family Responsibilities, 1981*
> *R. 195: Human Resources Development, 2004*

➜   See also **Access to employment; Division of labour; Marital status; Maternity leave; Parental leave; Paternity leave; Unpaid work**

Work–life balance

The term "work–life balance" refers not only to caring for dependent relatives, but also to "extracurricular" responsibilities or important life priorities. Work arrangements should be sufficiently flexible to enable workers of both sexes to undertake lifelong learning activities and further professional and personal development, not necessarily directly related to the worker's job.

However, for the purposes of the Convention and States' obligations in this rather vague area, the balance between work and family life is central to the principle and objectives of promoting equal opportunity. Issues related to the improvement of career opportunities, lifelong learning and other personal and professional development activities are considered to be secondary to the objective of promoting the more equal sharing between men and women of responsibilities in the family and household as well as in the workplace.

> *C. 156 and R. 165: Workers with Family Responsibilities, 1981*
> *R. 195: Human Resources Development, 2004*

➜   See also **Education; Family responsibilities, workers with; Work–family balance**

Workers on temporary contracts

→   See **Atypical work; Casual work; Family responsibilities, families with; Flexibility of labour; Part-time work**

Workers' organizations

→   See **Trade unions**

Working time

→   See **Hours of work**

| Y

Youth employment

Youth employment of both young men and women is a growing cause of concern for policy-makers and planners around the world. Between 1995 and 2005, the global unemployment rate of young people aged 15–24 rose from 12.1 to 13.7 per cent (ILO, 2006a, p. 21, para. 63).[26] Young women's unemployment and underemployment rates are even higher than those of young men in many countries. When jobs are scarce, young women are more likely than young men to drop out of the labour force rather than report being unemployed, or to take up part-time or casual work when full-time work is not available.

The paths to obtaining decent work for young women are often steeper and more beset with obstacles than those for young men. Equity in access to basic education is improving under the influence of the third Millennium Development Goal, and in many countries girls outperform boys at school; but access to training and the formal labour market is often barred by traditions that encourage (or enforce) early marriage or motherhood, or restricted by discrimination based on sex. While the situation varies a great deal from country to country, some obstacles to securing decent work are common to all young women. They often fail to take advantage of training opportunities because of entry barriers, discrimination in the selection process and gender stereotyping. Stereotyping is particularly found in vocational guidance and counselling on the part of school staff or employment services. Young women are encouraged to train in household-related or care work, while young men are urged to go for high-skilled and modern technology-based training and employment. As a result, many young women still end up in relatively low-skilled and poorly paid occupations with little prospect of upward mobility.

Policy-makers and planners should tackle the specific obstacles faced by young women by:

*   providing vocational guidance, counselling and placement services appropriate to young women's needs and capabilities;

*   facilitating girls' access to education and training in non-traditional subjects;

---

[26] Based on KILM figures.

- encouraging young women to choose training for jobs with better long-term earnings and prospects;

- collecting gender-sensitive data and improving labour market information systems to inform policy.

At the same time, the specific problems of boys and young men looking for work should not be ignored. When young men fail to find work and become discouraged, they do not even have work in the home to turn to and are more likely to be drawn into drug use and dealing, crime and violence.

In the framework of reporting progress towards the achievement of the Millennium Development Goals, the ILO takes the lead in reporting on trends concerning the employment rate among young people aged 15–24.

C. 111 and R. 111: Discrimination (Employment and Occupation), 1958
C. 122 and R. 122: Employment Policy, 1964
R. 169: Employment Policy (Supplementary Provisions), 1984
R. 195: Human Resources Development, 2004

➔ See also **Access to employment; Child labour; Education; Employment policy and promotion; Human resources development; Millennium Development Goals; Non-traditional occupations; Occupational segregation; Vocational guidance; Vocational training**

Bibliography

Basi, T. 2006. *Women working in call centres in India: Exploited workers or active agents in the new global economy?*, paper presented at the seminar, *Key challenges for research on women and the new economy in the 21st century*, Leeds University, Leeds, 30 June (Leeds).

Chappell, D. and di Martino, V. 2006. *Violence at work* (Geneva, ILO).

Coyle, A. 2006. *Structures of work and narratives of agency in women's call centres in the UK and India*, paper given at the seminar, Key challenges, Leeds University, Leeds, 30 June (Leeds).

Daly, M. (ed.). 2001. *Care work: The quest for security* (Geneva: ILO).

Daza, J.L. 2005. "Labour inspection and the informal economy: The global challenges of labour inspection", in *Labour Education*, Vol. 3/4, No. 140/141, pp. 15–21.

Elder, S. and Schmidt, D. 2004. *Global employment trends for women 2004* (Geneva: ILO).

European Commission (EC), Directorate-General for Employment, Industrial Relations and Social Affairs. 1998. *One hundred words for equality: A glossary of terms on equality between women and men* (Luxembourg).

–, EU Expert Group on Gender, Social Inclusion and Employment (EGGSIE). 2005. *Reconciliation of work and private life: Comparative review of thirty European countries* (Luxembourg).

European Foundation for the Improvement of Living and Working Conditions (Eurofound). 2007. "Telework", in *European Industrial Relations Dictionary*. Available at: http://www.eurofound.eu.

Hepple, B. 2001. "Equality and empowerment for decent work", in *International Labour Review*, Vol. 140, No. 1, pp. 5–18.

Hodges-Aeberhard, J. 1996. "Sexual harassment in employment: Recent judicial and arbitral trends", in *International Labour Review*, Vol. 135, No. 5, pp. 499–533.

–. 1999. *Policy and legal issues relating to HIV/AIDS and the world of work* (Geneva, ILO).

International Atomic Energy Agency (IAEA). 2004. *International Basic Safety Standards for protection against ionizing radiation and for the safety of radiation sources*, Safety Series No. 115-1 (Vienna).

International Labour Organization (ILO). 1985. *Official Bulletin*, Vol. 68, Ser. A (Geneva).

–. 1988. *Equality in Employment and Occupation, General Survey by the Committee of Experts on the Application of Conventions and Recommendations*, International Labour Conference, 75th Session, Geneva, 1988 (Geneva).

–. 1992. *General Report of the Committee of Experts on the Application of Conventions and Recommendations*, International Labour Conference, 79th Session, Geneva, 1992 (Geneva).

–. 1993a. *Bulletin of Labour Statistics* (Geneva).

–. 1993b. *General survey of the reports on the Workers with Family Responsibilities Convention and Recommendation*, III (3B), International Labour Conference, 80th Session, Geneva, 1993 (Geneva).

–. 1996. *Equality in employment and occupation*, Report III (4B), International Labour Conference, 83rd Session, Geneva, 1996 (Geneva).

–. 1997. P*rotection of workers' personal data: An ILO code of practice* (Geneva).

–, South-East Asia and the Pacific Multidisciplinary Team (SEAPAT). 1998. "Gender issues in the world of work", in *ILO/SEAPAT's OnLine Gender Learning & Information Module*. Available at: http://www.ilo.org/public/english/region/asro/mdtmanila/training/unit2/ipecgcdw.htm.

–. 1999. *Decent work*, Report of the Director-General, International Labour Conference, 87th Session, Geneva, 1999 (Geneva).

–. 2000. "Gender issues in social security and social protection", *Gender Mainstreaming in Technical Cooperation Projects for Social and Labour Spheres*, International Seminar, St. Petersburg, 2000 (St. Petersburg).

–. 2001a. *An ILO code of practice on HIV/AIDS in the world of work* (Geneva).

–. 2001b. *Report of the Director-General: Stopping forced labour. Global report under the follow-up to the ILO Declaration on Fundamental Principles and Rights at Work*, I (B), International Labour Conference, 89th Session, Geneva, 2001 (Geneva).

–, Gender Promotion Programme. 2001. *Realizing decent work for older women workers* (Geneva).

–. 2002a. *Report of the Committee on the Informal Economy*, Provisional Record 25, International Labour Conference, 90th Session, Geneva, 2002 (Geneva).

–. 2002b. *World Employment Report 2001: Life at work in the information economy* (Geneva).

–. 2003. *Report of the Director-General: Time for equality at work. Global report under the follow-up to the ILO Declaration on Fundamental Principles and Rights at Work*, I (B), International Labour Conference, 91st Session, Geneva, 2003 (Geneva).

–. 2004a. *Global employment trends for women*, 2004 (Geneva).

–. 2004b. *Leave and family responsibilities*. TRAVAIL Information Sheet No. WT 6 (Geneva). Available at: http://www.ilo.org/travail.

–. 2004c. *On-call work and "zero hours" contracts*. Conditions of Work and Employment Programme Information Sheet No. WT-15. (Geneva). Available at: http://www.ilo.org/condtrav.

—. 2004d. *Report of the Committee of Experts on the Application of Conventions and Recommendations. Promoting employment: Policies, skills, enterprises*, Report III (1B), International Labour Conference, 92nd Session, Geneva, 2004 (Geneva).

—. 2004e. *Shift Work*, TRAVAIL Information Sheet No. WT-8 (Geneva). Available at: http://www.ilo.org/travail.

—. 2004f. *Tripartite consultation: Ratify and apply Convention No. 144*, InFocus Programme on Social Dialogue, Labour Law and Labour Administration (Geneva).

—. 2004g. *Working time and health*. TRAVAIL Information Sheet No. WT-1 (Geneva). Available at http://ilo.org/travail.

—, World Commission on the Social Dimension of Globalization. 2004h. *A fair globalization: Creating opportunities for all* (Geneva).

—, Bureau for Employers' Activities. 2005. *Employers' organizations taking the lead on gender equality* (Geneva).

—. 2005a. *Manual for drafting ILO instruments* (Geneva). Also available at: http://www.ilo.org/public/english/bureau/leg.

—. 2005b. *Report of the Director-General: A global alliance against forced labour. Global report under the follow-up to the ILO Declaration on Fundamental Principles and Rights at Work*, I (B), International Labour Conference, 93rd Session, Geneva, 2005 (Geneva).

—. 2006a. *Report of the Director-General: Changing patterns in the world of work*, Report I (C), International Labour Conference, 95th Session, Geneva, 2006 (Geneva).

—. 2006b. *The employment relationship*, Report V (1), International Labour Conference, 95th Session, Geneva, 2006 (Geneva).

—. 2006c. *Report of the Director-General: The end of child labour: Within reach. Global Report under the Follow-up to the ILO Declaration on Fundamental Principles and Rights at Work*, I (B), International Labour Conference, 95th Session, Geneva, 2006 (Geneva).

—. 2006d. *The role of the ILO in technical cooperation*, Provisional Record 19 (166), International Labour Conference, 95th Session, Geneva, 2006 (Geneva).

—. 2007. *Global employment trends for women: brief*, March 2007 (Geneva).

Jhabvala, R. and Sinha, S. 2006. "Social protection for women workers in the informal economy", in *Comparative Labor Law and Policy Journal*, Vol. 27, No. 2, pp. 167–185.

Last, P.A. 1997. "Women's health", in J.M. Stellman (ed.): *Encyclopaedia of Occupational Health and Safety*, Vol. 1 (Geneva, ILO): pp. 15.48–15.52.

McCann, D. 2005. *Working time laws: A global perspective* (Geneva, ILO).

Messing, K and Östlin, P. 2006. *Gender equality, work and health: A review of the evidence* (Geneva, WHO).

Organisation for Economic Co-operation and Development (OECD). 1998. *DAC Sourcebook on concepts and approaches linked to gender equality* (Paris). Available at: http://www.oecd.org/dac.

Paul, J. 2004. *Healthy beginnings: Guidance on safe maternity at work* (Geneva: ILO).

Rodgers, G. 1989. "Precarious work in Western Europe: The state of the debate", in G. Rodgers and J. Rodgers (eds): *Precarious jobs in labour market regulation: The growth of atypical employment in Western Europe* (Geneva, ILO), pp. 1–16.

Séguret, M.-C. 1997. "Maternity protection in legislation", in J.M. Stellman (ed.): *Encyclopaedia of Occupational Health and Safety*, Vol. 1 (Geneva, ILO), pp. 9.22–9.26.

South Asian Association for Regional Cooperation (SAARC). 2002. "SAARC Eleventh Summit held in Kathmandu", *SAARC Press Release*. 9 January 2002. Available at: http://www.saarc-sec.org/old/11summit.htm.

Trebilcock, A. 2004. "International labour standards and the informal economy", in J.-C. Javillier, B. Gernigon and G. Politakis (eds): *Les norms internationales du travail: un patrimoine pour l'avenir*, Mélanges en l'honneur de Nicolas Valticos (Geneva: ILO), pp. 585–613.

UN Division for the Advancement of Women (UNDAW). 2003. *The role of men and boys in achieving gender equality*. Report of the Expert Group Meeting, Brasilia, 21–24 Oct. 2003.

UN Economic and Social Council (ECOSOC). 1997. *Mainstreaming the gender perspective into all policies and programmes in the United Nations system*, Agreed Conclusions 1997/2, in A/52/3/Rev. 1.

United Nations (UN), Population Division. 2007. *World Population Prospects: The 2006 revision population database*. Available at: http://esa.un.org/unpp/.

Working with VDUs (1998), in *International Occupational Safety and Health Information Centre (CIS) Bibliography* (Suffolk: Health and Safety Executive).

Further resources

Information on equal opportunities and non-discriminatory practices in different countries and systems can be obtained from the ILO in a number of ways.

ILO web sites

Access to further relevant data is provided at various places on the ILO's web site indicated below. All the web addresses cited were correct at 28 June 2007. If you encounter difficulties in accessing any of them, go to www.ilo.org and follow links to the department you require.

Bureau for Gender Equality: http://www.ilo.org/gender.

Standards and fundamental principles and rights at work: http://www.ilo.org/standards.

Social Dialogue, Labour Law and Labour Administration Department (DIALOGUE): http://www.ilo.org/dialogue.

Conditions of Work and Employment Programme (TRAVAIL): http://www.ilo.org/protection/condtrav.

Contains information sheet series and other resources on working time and work organization; wages and incomes; work and family (including maternity protection); working conditions; and workplace violence and harassment (including sexual harassment).

Programme on Safety and Health at Work and the Environment (SAFEWORK): http://www.ilo.org/public/english/protection/safework.

Contains resources on gender and occupational health and safety issues. The SOLVE programme can be accessed from SAFEWORK, under "Workers' Well-being".

International Institute for Labour Studies: http://www.ilo.org/bureau/inst.

ILOLEX, database of ILO Conventions and Recommendations: http://www.ilo.org/ilolex/english/index.htm.

NATLEX, database of national labour legislation: http://www.ilo.org/dyn/natlex/natlex_browse.home.

ILO Bureau of Statistics: http://www.ilo.org/bureau/stat/index.htm.

KILM (Key Indicators of the Labour Market) database: http://www.ilo.org/public/english/employment/strat/kilm/index.htm. Full service available on subscription.

Resources on the informal economy: http://www.ilo.org/infeco.

Bureau for Workers' Activities (ACTRAV): http://www.ilo.org/dialogue/actrav/genact/gender/gendtu/.

Contains information on trade unions and gender equality issues.

WEDGE web site on women's entrepreneurship and gender equality: http://www.ilo.org/dyn/empent/empent.Portal?p_prog=S&p_subprog=WE.

ILO Encyclopaedia of Occupational Safety and Health, Fourth ed.: http://www.ilo.org/encyclopedia/.

CD-ROM resources

The ILO's International Training Centre in Turin has developed a hypertext version of the *Women Workers' Rights Information Kit* on CD-Rom. The English prototype version is already available and may be requested from: Women in Development Programme, International Training Centre of the ILO, Viale Maestri del Lavoro 10, 10127 Turin, Italy (Fax: +39 011 6936 350; email: WID@itcilo.it).

The Bureau for Gender Equality has compiled the ILO's legislation on gender equality in *Decent work and gender equality: Selected ILO Conventions and Recommendations for promoting gender equality in the world of work*, available in both hard copy and CD-ROM formats.

The Social Dialogue, Labour Law and Labour Administration Department (DIALOGUE) publishes *Labour Legislation Guidelines*, by Arturo Bronstein and Vladislav Egorov (Second ed. 2003) in both hard copy and CD-ROM formats.

Further reading

Anker, Richard. Gender and jobs: Sex segregation of occupations in the world. Geneva: ILO, 1998.

ILO, Bureau for Gender Equality. 2000. *Decent work for women: An ILO proposal to accelerate the implementation of the Beijing Platform for Action* (Geneva).

—. 2000. *Globalizing Europe: Decent work in the information economy.* Report of the Director General, Sixth European Regional Meeting, Geneva 2000 (Geneva).

—. 2002. *Women and men in the informal sector: A statistical picture* (Geneva).

—. 2006. *Gender equality and decent work: Selected ILO Conventions and Recommendations promoting gender equality* (Geneva).

European Commission, Directorate-General for Employment, Industrial Relations and Social Affairs. 1998. *One hundred words for equality: A glossary of terms on equality between women and men* (Luxembourg).

Herrell, I. et al. 2003. *Guide to mainstreaming gender into technical cooperation projects on social dialogue* (Geneva: ILO).

Hodges-Aeberhard, J. 2004. *Guidelines on addressing HIV/AIDS in the workplace through employment and labour law.* (Geneva: ILO).

Lim, L.L. et al. 2002. *Promoting gender equality: A resource kit for trade unions* (Geneva: ILO).

March, C., Smythe, I. and Mukhopadhyay, M. 1999. *A guide to gender analysis frameworks* (Oxford: Oxfam).

Mata-Greenwood, A. 2000. *Incorporating gender issues in labour statistics* (Geneva: ILO).

Olney, S. et al. 1998. *Gender equality: a guide to collective bargaining* (Geneva: ILO).

– and Rueda, M. 2005. *Convention 154: Promoting collective bargaining* (Geneva: ILO).

Reinhart, A. 1999. *Addressing sexual harassment in the workplace – a management information booklet* (Geneva: ILO).

Wirth, L. 2004. *Breaking through the glass ceiling; Women in management,* Second ed. (Geneva: ILO).